SOCIAL JUSTICE RE-EXAMINED
dilemmas and solutions for the
classroom teacher

Social Justice Re-examined is about making a difference in classrooms and schools. It shows that 'you do not have to be a superhero to be a teacher for social justice'. There is a powerful voice in this book of real classrooms and real teachers which lends it a sense of authenticity.

This very rich collection of chapters fills gaps that are simply not addressed in other books. It shows that education is not neutral but involves a contested set of values and ethical perspectives where there are winners and losers. It will help empower new and experienced teachers in moving towards a socially just future, and holding onto a sense of joy in teaching.

Professor Meg Maguire, King's College London

A clear message is to be found here: all of us can make choices about what we teach and how we teach. The book provides a considered discussion about what social justice means and how it is relevant to every classroom.

The time is ripe for thinking about teaching as an activist profession. We can reshape the lives of our students by giving them the tools to challenge and change their world.

Claire Chalmers, young teacher, City of Edinburgh

This is an extremely important, valuable and timely book, full of practical and down-to-earth guidance which all teachers will find useful. It is concerned with supporting children and young people who are disadvantaged by inequalities and unfairness in wider society.

It deals with sensitive and controversial issues connected with diversity, identity and equality. The book's answers are not only practical and immediately helpful, they are firmly and impressively based in theory and reflection, and in sound educational values and principles.

Robin Richardson, former director of the Runnymede Trust

The contributors write from a contemporary perspective which recognises the multi-dimensionality of social justice and the many challenges to a socially just education.

The writing style is personal and passionate. It will speak to teachers and student teachers. I shall certainly recommend it on the courses I teach, to help undergraduate and postgraduate students answer the questions: What is education for? and What can I do about it?

Professor Geri Smyth, University of Strathclyde

SOCIAL JUSTICE RE-EXAMINED
dilemmas and solutions for the classroom teacher

*edited by Rowena Arshad,
Terry Wrigley and
Lynne Pratt*

Trentham Books

Stoke on Trent, UK and Sterling, USA

Trentham Books Limited
Westview House   22883 Quicksilver Drive
734 London Road   Sterling
Oakhill   VA 20166-2012
Stoke on Trent   USA
Staffordshire
England ST4 5NP

First published 2012

British Library Cataloguing-in-Publication Data
A catalogue record for this book is available from the British Library

ISBN 978-1-85856-507-1

Designed and typeset by Trentham Books Ltd, Chester and Printed and bound in Great Britain by 4edge Limited, Hockley

Contents

Section 2
Learning from school and classroom situations

Foreword

Ian Menter, University of Oxford

In 2010 I led a team which carried out a study of teacher education for the Scottish Government. We reviewed literature on teacher education in the first decade of the 21st century (Menter *et al*, 2010), and were able to identify four different understandings of teacher professionalism:

- the effective teacher
- the reflective teacher
- the enquiring teacher
- the transformative teacher.

Each of these models has important aspects. Teachers clearly need to be *effective* in enabling children to learn the skills, knowledge and understanding that are set down in the curriculum. It is also desirable for teachers to be *reflective* in the sense that they can evaluate their own practice and thereby improve it. An *enquiring* teacher may go a step further and start applying simple research techniques to their practices in order to make such improvements more systematic. But what then is meant by the term *transformative* when applied to teachers? Well, one answer to that question emerges clearly from this book.

Every chapter in this book is in some way or other making the case for teachers to be conscious of the values that underlie their professional work and to base their developing practice on those values. The particular set of values they are concerned with can be summarised as 'social justice'. This term is especially resonant in Scotland where most of the book's authors are based. Having re-established its own Parliament in

1999, Scotland has sought to imbue its political, social and cultural life with the humane values of fairness, compassion and wisdom, all key elements of social justice. The quest for fairness and equality is not a straightforward one, either in society at large or within education. Indeed, since one of the purposes of a state education system is to prepare young people to take up particular roles in society both in their homes and in their workplaces – in other words to prepare young people for *different* life experiences with *different* rewards and *different* levels of satisfaction, it could be argued that the education system itself is there to legitimate *in*equality in society. (And we should not forget that some children's families actually have sufficient wealth to buy a supposedly superior education for their children through a private school system that runs in parallel. Can that be socially just, we may ask?).

These kinds of questions have occupied the minds of philosophers over many centuries and have been a key concern within the sociology of education as it developed during the past century. No doubt these important debates will continue. In the meantime, teachers in schools are working with children, shaping their futures in significant ways. And so it is that the teacher who seeks to promote social justice is faced with considerable challenges both within their own classroom and also in terms of the influences they may have in the wider community.

In the 1960s Neil Postman and Charles Weingartner wrote a book entitled *Teaching as a Subversive Activity* (Postman and Weingartner, 1971). This title, and others like it, caught the imagination of many young student teachers of that time who felt a strong desire to confront inequality and social injustice through their work. Many of these students soon found themselves teaching in communities where poverty and unemployment were rife. The 1970s and 1980s saw a wave of anti-discriminatory activity in education, with groups being established to challenge racism and sexism in education and subsequently movements to support the rights of learners of all sexualities and abilities. Such teachers and the networks they formed often worked closely with and through their trade unions, and through various community groups in the areas where they worked.

Important though these developments were, at least two major difficulties emerged. The first was that the emphasis on disadvantaged communities meant that *other* communities tended to be seen as 'normal', so not requiring an equivalent 'special' approach. There is a reference to this issue in the title of Chris Gaine's book *No Problem Here* (1988). Gaine's work was specifically about multicultural and antiracist education and he was drawing attention to the fact that it was all too easy for schools and teachers in predominantly white communities to ignore or at least play down the importance of education for racial equality. The call for the 'mainstreaming' of education for equality was also echoed in the moves towards the integration of children with special learning needs out of 'special schools' and into mainstream schools, a process which would require changes in the mainstream schools. Moves such as these also gave rise to a new language of social justice which emphasised inclusion and diversity as positive features, not just overcoming exclusion and discrimination.

The second difficulty which emerged in the 1970s and 1980s came from politicians. With the rise to dominance of New Right politics, largely associated in the UK with Margaret Thatcher's governments of the 1980s, there was a strong call for education to 'return to basics'. The creation of a largely traditionalist National (and some would say nationalistic) Curriculum in England in 1988 was just one element in a widespread attack on education as a means of social transformation. In one infamous speech Thatcher denounced such approaches, making fun of anti racist mathematics – 'whatever that may be!'

However, these difficulties with educational policies concerning social justice did not of course mean that the issues which gave rise to them had disappeared. On the contrary, as Wilkinson and Pickett (2010) and Dorling (2011) have demonstrated, British society has become far less equal and social injustice has increased. Can teachers ignore these matters? One of the teachers quoted in Rowena Arshad's opening chapter says, 'I am here to teach, not to be a social worker'. But can teaching be effective if it does not challenge injustice?

The underlying argument for social justice as a foundation for teaching is multi-faceted. Here let me pick out just two issues.

First, we do have to return to philosophy and to ask 'What is Education for?' So much emphasis in political discourse over recent years has been placed on the economic benefits of education – enabling our nation to compete in what is described as an increasingly competitive globalised world – that the social, cultural and political benefits of education have been downplayed. Education in a democracy must play a part in sustaining the appropriate values of that democracy – in other words what is required (in part) is education *for* democracy. The values of citizenship and of human rights are key elements in sustaining such an approach.

But second, in a very direct sense, social justice is deeply embedded within the processes of learning and teaching in schools. Teaching and learning have been shown to be much more effective in classrooms where teachers and learners are fully respected. Indeed trust and respect are fundamental underpinnings of effective learning. Some of the policies affecting teachers and learners in many education systems show little trust or respect for teachers or learners. One can think here of punitive inspection systems, the 'naming and shaming' of schools, the promotion of crude 'league tables' producing simplistic comparisons between schools, the reductionist approaches to measuring 'teacher performance', or indeed the crude imposition of particular teaching techniques, especially in literacy. These reveal a new world order that does little to improve the quality of teaching or learning.

The message that comes through from this book is that education and schooling do *not* have to be like this. Teaching can and should be an activist profession (Sachs, 2003a). Through the informed and carefully planned work of teachers, education can be an empowering and democratising experience for learners. It can provide them with the skills and understanding not only to make informed choices and decisions about their own life trajectories, but to consider the wider contribution they may make to the development of their community and society. Such approaches do create tensions, friction, and even dissent and conflict at times. But if we are to have an education system fit for the range of economic, ecological and political challenges which face the world in the 21st century, then we should heed the call for education for social justice that emerges so strongly from the chapters in this book.

References

Dorling, D (2011) *So You Think You Know About Britain?* London: Constable

Gaine, C (1988) *No Problem Here.* London: Nelson Thornes

Menter, I, Hulme, M, Elliot, D and Lewin, J (2010) *Literature Review on Teacher Education in the 21st Century.* Social Research series. Edinburgh: The Scottish Government

Postman, N and Weingartner, C (1971) *Teaching as a Subversive Activity.* Harmondsworth: Penguin Books

Sachs, J (2003a) *The Activist Teaching Profession.* London: Open University Press

Wilkinson, R and Pickett, K (2010) *The Spirit Level: why equality is better for everyone.* London: Penguin

Terminology

The chapters in this book were written by a mix of English and Scottish authors, and because the two education systems differ, readers will find slight differences in the terminology used.

School years in England are numbered from Year 1 (the start of primary) through to Year 13 (age 18). Primary schools end at Year 6 (abbreviated as Y6), and the compulsory years of secondary school run from Year 7 to Year 11 (five years).

Primary schools in Scotland run from Primary 1 to Primary 7 (abbreviated as P1 to P7), and pupils are slightly older when they move to secondary. Secondary schools run from S1 to S6, with the first four years being compulsory.

In England, the compulsory years of schooling are divided into 'key stages': KS1 and KS2 in primary, and KS3 and KS4 in secondary. There is no equivalent concept in Scotland. Public examinations are also different: for example, the gateway to university is A-levels in English schools and Highers in Scotland.

Many teachers and educational writers in England prefer to use the word student rather than *pupil*, especially in secondary schools. In Scotland *pupil* is almost universal. This does not imply any difference in how young people are regarded by their teachers.

The English *National Curriculum* has had its parallel in Scotland in terms of a strongly defined set of content as well as skills. Scotland is in the middle of a major curriculum reform called *Curriculum for Excellence* (CfE), which allows teachers rather more freedom to make decisions and respond to pupils' needs. Overall the English education system imposes more disciplinarian control on teachers through Ofsted (the inspection agency), exam results published as 'league tables', and ultimately closure and privatised management if results are below average. This can affect teachers' confidence in taking initiatives relating to social justice.

The one-year postgraduate course to prepare graduates for teaching is called the PGCE in England but PGDE in Scotland. The term Initial Teacher Education is preferred in Scotland, rather than Teacher Training, to reflect a stronger theoretical basis.

Hopefully, none of these differences will prevent readers from recognising the situations and issues they find in this book.

Section 1

Social justice: what has it got to do with me?

1

Shaping practice: the impact of personal values and experiences

Rowena Arshad

We can educate the next generation to solve many of our problems if we are courageous enough to free them from our own prejudices and anxieties. (Charlotte Epstein, teacher, quoted in Rudduck, 1986:11)

This book is about encouraging teachers to engage proactively with social justice. It argues that teachers who engage with social justice issues are better able to offer pupils an academically rigorous education that prepares them for being a confident individual and an effective contributor both in society as a whole and in the world of work. Teachers who are aware of these issues do not just help their pupils to read, write and attain but are more able to provide their pupils with a conducive learning environment which allows each pupil to maximise their potential.

Research suggests that teacher expectations can be pivotal in influencing pupil motivation (Macbeath, 1998; Gillborn and Youdell, 2000). Just think back to your school days and you can probably identify the teachers who motivated you, the teacher who developed your interest in a subject or topic, the ones that bored you and made you think about skipping class, the ones who everyone knew did not really care and so on. Research also tells us that teachers do make a difference when they explicitly address issues of social justice with their peers and with pupils (Connell, 1985; Richardson, 1990; Wrigley, 2000; Kehily, 2002).

Russo (2004) suggests that for teachers to engage in social justice, there are two essential concepts to understand. The first is that teachers for social justice need to explicitly acknowledge that injustice exists in society and that, for various reasons, some people are more privileged than others. Russo argues that it is important for teachers to understand 'how privilege operates, how disadvantage (or marginalisation) occurs, how advantage or disadvantage is cyclical in nature'.

The second concept is that teachers need to believe they can be change agents by interrupting disadvantage and thinking about what they teach and how they teach. One of the most influential educators and social thinkers of the late twentieth century, Paulo Freire, suggested that education can be used either to domesticate or to liberate. Teachers can be agents of change or they can be guardians of the status quo.

For example, by a subtle change of wording, a teacher can change the tone of a sentence or situation.

> The *congested* streets of Mumbai...
> The *bustling* streets of Mumbai...

The term 'congested' gives the image of excessive crowding and a somewhat chaotic situation. However, 'bustling' creates a picture of a noisy but acceptably exciting and busy situation. Values can be imparted unconsciously through the choice of word or content of what we teach.

The impact of a teacher who is prepared to be bold and challenging can be seen in the person of Jane Elliot. Many of you will have heard of the classroom experiment where pupils were divided by the colour of their eyes to 'blue eyed' and 'brown eyed' groups. The groups were treated differently: one group was privileged over the other (eg. given longer break times, given more praise). It is not the experiment itself that I am concerned with but the impact of her teaching on those children. Jane Elliot brought her students back fifteen years later and it was clear that her lessons about justice had a long lasting effect.[1] Another important lesson that Jane Elliot learned was that on the day that the one group was being discriminated against, their test scores went down, and on the next day when they were being given privileges, their test scores went up. These test scores were sent to Stanford University's Psychology Department for analysis and academics were taken aback at the speed at which the pupils' academic achievement was being affected by the gain or loss of esteem.

The chapters in Section 1 of this book should assist you in considering why it is important that you to take on board social justice issues as part of your thinking and practice. This section also provides you with the conceptual framework within which to think about these issues – see Chapter 3. The chapters in Section 2 discuss how a particular characteristic such as gender, class, disability or social circumstances (eg. poverty) can create advantage or disadvantage. Each chapter also provides ideas of how teachers can interrupt cycles of disadvantage in these different areas.

A tale of two students...

I have been lecturing about issues of justice and discrimination for nearly twenty years. I want to start by reflecting on comments from two second-year teacher education students whom I had the pleasure to teach – Gina and Robbie.

Robbie asked me why he needed to take social justice seriously as he was neither female or gay nor was he from a minority ethnic or lower income group. He acknowledged that he might develop a disability as he was active in sports and could therefore sustain an injury, so he stated that issues pertaining to physical disability might be of relevance to him. Robbie said that he had never been on the receiving end of discrimination and did not understand the issue in a 'real-life' sense. He stated that he was 'training to be a teacher, not a social worker.'

Gina was in my tutorial group and felt strongly that she 'treated all her pupils the same' and therefore did not exclude or discriminate against anyone. She felt that discrimination would not take place in her class because she was sensitive and inclusive and would not tolerate prejudice or prejudicial views. Gina acknowledged that discrimination does occur in society. However, she believed that most pupils developed prejudiced ideas either from the home or in the community and that the problem lay with society rather than within a school. She accepted that it was important for teachers to be aware of these problems but did not feel the need for teachers to 'go over the top'.

It is encouraging that both Gina and Robbie were able to speak up during lectures and tutorials as their comments allowed me as the tutor to explore the points being made within their group.

Let's unpack Robbie's points first. Why indeed would someone who is unlikely to experience a particular form of disadvantage invest time, emotional or intellectual energy in engaging with these issues? Hollway (1984) suggests that for members of dominant groups to become interested in minority cultures or different ways of thinking, they need to develop a reason to 'invest' time and intellect in these matters. Finding these reasons or personal rewards can be a challenge as they are often not monetary.

Gaine (2005) offers two motives as to why teachers might become interested in social justice. Firstly, he suggests that such investment is sometimes given because of a 'pragmatic motive'. Teachers in this category take issues relating to social justice forward because the law and their professional body (eg. the General Teaching Council) require them to do so. They often do just enough to comply with legislation and their professional framework but view these concerns as add-ons to their core duties of teaching and assessing.

Gaine offers a second reason which he calls the 'principle motive'. The principled position is where teachers believe it is their duty to provide fair treatment to their pupils and enable equality of opportunity as much as they can. For many teachers in this category, it is a matter of principle to grapple with the human cost of discrimination. They recognise that education makes an important contribution in reducing that cost.

As a white, able-bodied, middle-class male Robbie perceived social justice to be of benefit to others but not to himself. In a way, he could afford to be indifferent. For someone like Robbie, Gaine's pragmatic motive may well be the starting point. However, if he is to become an effective teacher for an increasingly diverse pupil population, he will need to develop empathy for his pupils as well as an understanding of how his own privileged position might influence his values and perceptions of reality. Failure to do so would likely result in him not doing the best for his pupils and failing in his duty as a twenty-first century professional.

For most teachers, the reward is not one of financial gain but lies in their belief that they can make a difference. In Chapters 2 and 4 of this book, Laura Mitchell and Helen Knowles discuss how classroom teachers have made a difference by concerning themselves with social justice.

Gina's belief that treating all her pupils in the same way meant she was being equal and fair is at best naïve and at worst potentially damaging and discriminatory. Gina's experiences of life to date, including her personal experiences of family, friends and childhood and previous experiences of learning, both positive and negative, would have shaped who she is as a student teacher, and those experiences will play a part in shaping her professional identity, orientation and practice.

Studies of teachers' personal and professional beliefs have found a correlation between them (Connell, 1985; Smith *et al*, 1997; Gaine, 2001; Pearce, 2005). Causey *et al* (1999:34) describe this prior knowledge as the 'filters' or 'intuitive screens' through which teachers develop their thinking on particular issues.

If Gina is to do her best for her pupils, she needs to be able to reflect critically and constructively on these experiences and consider how they might have shaped her values and views of different people, issues and even approaches to teaching. For example, if she comes from a home with easy access to a computer and sets her homework tasks to generally include research on the internet, how might this impact on those pupils in the class who have either no home to go back to – they are in care – or limited computer access?

Some influences as told to us by teachers

As part of my doctorate research from 2006 to 2008, I wanted to find out what contributed to developing a teacher's interest in issues of equality and social justice. I worked with nine teachers (six women, three men) in Scotland from both the primary and secondary sector. Their ages varied from 28 to 65; two identified themselves as being from a visible minority ethnic group and one as having a disability. Each person was interviewed several times over a six-month period. The teachers selected were recognised by fellow teachers as people who were prepared to champion issues of social justice. Some teachers were identified as part of my work and some were recommended for the study by fellow teachers.

The study identified the following themes as some of the influences that shaped teacher interest in social justice:

- the influence of family and home
- personal experiences of discrimination
- the influence of religion
- the tapestry of self (multiple identities)
- being part of the 'other'.

As you read on, you may wish to reflect on whether any of these influences match your own experience or whether you draw from different influences.

Family and home

All the teachers interviewed found family to be an important learning source. Stone (1988:7, cited by Clandinin and Connelly, 2000:113) suggested that 'the particular human chain we're part of is central to our individual identity'. J Gary Knowles (1992) noted that early childhood experiences, along with early teacher role models and previous teaching experiences, were most important in the teacher's formation of an 'image of self.'

The family unit, particularly mother and father, were viewed by the majority as important early educators and socialising agents:

> My mum and dad had a greengrocer's which was beside the hospital. There was a lot of people there – even from other parts of Europe. My dad went out of his way to order, what was then classed as exotic fruits and veg because people had come in an asked him. It was just wee things like that I picked up on. (Teacher C, male)

> He [father] had a job which had him travelling around the Highlands. In those days you used to get lots of hitchhikers and he used to give them lifts. At weekends when I was out with him we would pick up hitchhikers. You would learn about other people's backgrounds from that. Later on they converted their house into a guesthouse and there was a wide-ranging clientele. (Teacher G, male)

Some of the teachers interviewed had chosen to move away from the values and attitudes they had been brought up with. One teacher talked about her family being 'quite a racist family, a very white Scottish male-dominated traditional family...' and while she was loyal to her family, particularly her father, she knew the prejudices they held were not ones she wanted to share.

Other teachers recalled family situations where being the *other* incurred hostility.

> My mum who is Catholic married my dad who was Protestant. People have referred to her as the black sheep of the family... Then when I was about 18, my gran died and it was the first time he [father] had ever been in my gran's house. ... – (Teacher F, female)

Teacher F's family grew up in a context where sectarian divides were a reality. These memories have fuelled Teacher F's commitment to tackling injustice and discrimination. While there was no overt home discussion on matters related to sectarianism, her mother, who she named as an influential character in her life, had taught her to stand up for herself and for what was right regardless of the context. This message of standing up for oneself has been interpreted by this teacher, at different stages of her life, as standing up for those less powerful, for others who cannot speak up for themselves and for human rights and justice:

> I've come to realise since a teenager I've been quite in people's faces and I know I have got people's backs up. Becoming a teacher I tried not to upset people as much as I typically have done. But if I hear someone say something that is unjust or unfair or things that aren't politically correct, I will speak up.

Teacher E grew up in an area that was largely homogeneous, certainly in terms of colour:

> There were very few children whose skin wasn't white in my schools. There were one or two children. So I don't think as a child or at university my friendship groups were very diverse, there were very few non-white faces...

Coming from homes where politics and social issues were discussed or experienced was an early contributory factor to developing teacher awareness and interest in social justice issues.

Personal experiences of discrimination

At least six of the nine teachers described examples either of personal experiences of discrimination or of having witnessed discrimination as they grew up. These experiences acted like bridges, helping these teachers make connections with other forms of injustice:

> It's probably due to me coming up here to Scotland when I was 7 years of age. So I was English, with an English accent, ... I tended to get picked on for my English accent ... Yeah and I remember my mum telling me how quickly I was trying to get rid of it, in order to merge. (Teacher C, male)

> I grew up and some people have this idyllic picture of living in a rural part of Scotland, well you knew the pecking order where you fitted in ... According to the society I lived in, I wasn't at the top, I wasn't one of the folk that paid for education but I wasn't at the bottom because I was well dressed. (Teacher A, female)

Some teachers in this study did not experience direct discrimination as children but were affected as they left the safety of their families and childhood. One teacher encountered gender discrimination at university:

> I was in a drama department studying drama and all of the lecturers were male, two-thirds of the students were female. There were elements of performance in the course and the opportunity for performance for women was absolutely limited. The opportunities for men were not limited in terms of what decisions were made. There was also a case of sexual harassment which I had to deal with and [it] just got blocked by the hierarchy. (Teacher E, female)

Others began to be affected by discrimination as they attempted to progress in their employment:

> I work in a university in the northern part of Country X [abroad] which is not where I originally come from. I'm from the south ... [With regards to] Promotion ... if you are not from the catchment area, it is very difficult to rise beyond maybe senior lecturer level. (Teacher B, female, visible minority ethnic)

Whilst having the experience counts, it is the attachment of meaning to that experience that produces really useful knowledge. Only when the experience connects to and positively influences the future does the knowledge it generates become of use. The experience of having undergone some form of discrimination enabled some teachers in this study to become more aware of issues of difference and how such difference can lead to discrimination.

The influence of religion

At least six teachers in the study identified their faith as a key influence on their commitment to social justice. The church was cited as an institution that shaped some teachers' identity and attitudes to fairness and justice:

> We went to the Catholic primary school. It's basically that, the values of the Catholic church of fairness and so on ... I think it ingrained in me ... a sense of fairness and one of the things I really hate is bullying of any kind. So it's not really just racism but discrimination of any kind. I don't like people being treated unfairly. (Teacher C, male)

The influence of the church or religion was not always positive however. Two teachers in particular questioned whether the church, as an establishment, or religions in general sat comfortably with the principles of equality and human rights:

> When I decided to marry my boyfriend I went to my minister, who had been my minister when I was growing up. He knew I wanted to be a missionary and I had just finished my teacher training ... So when I went to talk to the minister about getting married, he realised I was living with my boyfriend and said he wouldn't marry me. This was about six years ago and I was still attending church and ran youth groups. If this was such a condemnable sin, living with someone who really loves me and who I really love, I think Jesus would forgive this ... – (Teacher E, female)

Another teacher, who is a lesbian, felt that while lesbians and gay people would actively challenge issues like Islamophobia or sectarianism, people of faith did not always support her right to be a lesbian or the right to have a same-sex marriage. This made it difficult for her at times to empathise with people of faith.

Whether they were positive or negative, church and faith shaped some of these teachers' values and views on fairness, justice and difference. The teachers who are practising Christians have gone on to be proactive in their practice of teaching about other faiths and on tackling Islamophobia and antisemitism.

The tapestry of self

Alsup (2006) suggests that our personal experiences and material conditions influence how we construct not just our professional identity as teachers but also our professional orientation and practice.

Teacher A in my study grew up in a small rural town where, as she put it, 'you knew the pecking order where you fitted in.' The first in her family to move into tertiary education, she had never forgotten her roots. Teacher A's life became consumed with class inequality and in conversations with me she displayed a fair degree of intolerance for those she perceived as being from the 'upper middle classes.'

All the women teachers interviewed, regardless of their ethnic, age and social class groups, had stories about the impact of being a female in a man's world. Some knew from the outset that they did not wish to have their choices limited because of their gender, and while all grew up in loving homes there were tensions they had to grapple with. Quite a few talked about the traditionality of home life within the communities they grew up in.

While others were not affected by gender stereotyping, they were acutely conscious that it existed. In the case of Teacher F:

> I guess in terms of when I had my daughter because I try not to dress her always in pink, she always gets pink stuff, and just because she is a girl doesn't mean she has to wear pink ... I sometimes think if I had a boy next how much harder it would be for people if I dressed him in pink. People take it fairly well if I dress her in boys' clothes but how bothered people are if I say I'll put it away for the next baby. They always say, 'But you don't know what you're having next'. Well no I don't but I know it will be this size at some point so they can wear it. I wonder if people think that by dressing a boy in pink if it will make him gay.

These experiences gave the women teachers in the study a lasting sense of the injustices women can face in what is still a male-dominated world. Many have become involved in voluntary work or campaigns related to gender such as breast cancer awareness. Only one of the three male teachers in this study commented directly on how gender issues impacted on their personal lives. Teacher C found that his awareness of sexism and issues relating to sexual discrimination rose through discussion with his wife:

> Being married has helped, being with [my wife], she sees things differently as a woman and you realise things aren't fair. I think you carry on learning all the time.

Gender is one dimension of the tapestry of self. Other aspects that emerged from the conversations were those of ethnicity and nationality.

Being part of the 'other'

The experience of being different or the 'other' helped some teachers to begin to understand why it is important to promote equality and social justice. For these teachers addressing injustice took on a personal resonance. Teacher H found she had to confront a teacher in her school who was speaking negatively about some children speaking Punjabi. Teacher H is Asian and speaks Punjabi herself:

> They will say, 'Oh they are speaking Punjabi and I find it rude' or 'I've told them it's for the playground', or another teacher said to me, 'Oh I don't know why they aren't taken to another school and educated separately, it must be so frustrating for them to be in a school where they don't understand the language' ... A few weeks later I thought how should I raise this, so I took some literature into the staff room on the positives of bilingualism and this teacher again said, 'Well I find it rude', then another said the parents don't want them to speak their first language and all the teachers joined in this conversation. So I just thought I'd mention it to the Head then keep a low profile for a while.

When Teacher H's colleagues were talking about 'those' pupils, she clearly saw herself as part of *those* people. If her colleagues had persisted in being negative about pupils who do not speak English as their first language, it would have had a direct impact on her identity and self-esteem. This created an uncomfortable position for these teachers who knew they could well be perceived as part of the 'other'. The idea of *personal cost* is alluded to several times over the interviews with teachers who have been labelled *minority*.

While hearing about a potential homophobic incident involving some Primary 2 (Y2) pupils, Teacher E, who is a lesbian, felt she had to keep an eye on what happened next:

> What happened was a child in Primary 2 told her peers that she was a lesbian. Then the peers and the child responded as seeing that it was something bad but I don't know why the child said that in the first place. When I first heard it, I couldn't tell if it was a homophobic incident or not ... the teacher responded that [the children] don't know what it means. Yes, they are seeing it as something bad or distasteful but I don't know how it has

been dealt with before. The school doesn't have a clear line. If something racist was said teachers would think 'I have to do or say something about this' [but] they don't have that with homophobia. I'm at the point where I want to talk about this, not as staff but I think we need to have a line on it. We need to be good at it and have an agreement on it. I am doing it on my own in my classroom but I think we need to have an agreement on it.

The stories of teachers who saw themselves as part of the minority differed from those of the teachers who had not themselves faced systemic discrimination. Teachers who were from minority groups felt less able to walk away or be indifferent.

A different future

For teachers like Robbie and Gina, whose life experiences have not really engaged them to think of diversity, difference or discrimination, structured experiences will be needed to enable that thinking to develop.

At present, many teachers' capacities to understand why discrimination occurs and how to create the changes at classroom or institutional level which are necessary to promote equity, diversity and inclusion remain under-developed. This book intends to help student teachers and experienced teachers become the transformative and innovative educators they can and should be. That means engaging with key concepts like power, discrimination and oppression rather than being content with more palatable terms like inclusion, diversity and equal opportunities. It also means having the courage to stand up and be counted.

Ras (2004:5) suggests that teachers, 'unlike other less socially intense professions, must deal with their pupils' needs, moods and difficulties while satisfying externally defined goals'. As part of their profession, they are expected to mould the next generation into better citizens, as well as being 'technicians of education, presented with new curricula or standards and expected to be the tools of outcome production' (2004:6).

In the day-to-day reality of survival, taking social justice issues on board can be a tiring endeavour. However, challenging injustice and helping to create a better learning environment or world is something that everyone can contribute to. Cooper (2003:415) found that regardless of whether a teacher was black or white or in a denominational or non-denominational school, it was the teacher's belief in what is possible that mattered most. When studying the teachers' refusal to accept black children's scholastic underachievement, their commitment to educational opportunity and deep respect they had for black parents and the black community were the attributes that made them effective teachers.

In Chapter 3 Shereen Benjamin and Akwugo Emejulu talk about the importance of being 'explicit in our thinking about difference'. They go on to discuss the social and deficit models of difference. The social model approach moves away from a deficit mentality of 'blaming the victim'. It is an approach that works positively with difference rather than seeing difference as a problem.

Smyth (2004:25) talks about the importance of 'sustaining a pedagogical mindset with which to counter the unequal opportunity structures' as a way of ensuring a socially-just teaching practice and developing a socially just school. Smyth also reminds us that education is about more than just accountability, tests, numbers or targets; ultimately it is about how we assist pupils to 'decode the system', and create school cultures that generate trust and connections with pupils, parents and communities rather than distrust and detachment.

This book throws down a challenge to teachers of the twenty-first century become activist teachers with the commitment to stand up for justice and the courage to speak out rather than to stay silent. Sachs (2003) suggests that to become an activist teacher, the individual teacher must be politically astute and neither risk-averse nor risk-anxious. They should value social relations, move away from individualistic identities to a 'we' mentality and be prepared to question and, if needed, disrupt the norm. She further suggests that activist teachers tend to locate their work in a transformation agenda that requires change not just outside the school gates but within the school and within the classroom.

In his research Fullan (1993:12) found that teachers often say the reason they enter teaching is 'to make a difference in the lives of students'. If that is to be true then individual teachers must recognise the potency of personal power (Macdonald, 2007:132) – that is, the personal power they have to make the difference.

If you ever doubt the impact you can make, reflect on this African proverb:

If you think you are too small to make a difference,
try to sleep in a closed room with a mosquito ...

Note

1 Jane Elliot's reunion with her students can be seen at http://video.google.com/videoplay?docid=6189991712636113875 (view from the start or from 18 minutes to 28.15 minutes).

References

Alsup, J (2006) *Teacher Identity Discourses: negotiating personal and professional spaces.* New Jersey/Illinois: Lawrence Erlbaum Associates with the National Council of Teachers of English

Causey, V E, Thomas, C D and Armento, B J (1999) Cultural diversity is basically a foreign term to me: the challenges of diversity for preservice teacher education. *Teaching and Teacher Education* 16 p33-45

Clandinin, D J and Connelly, FM (2000) *Narrative Inquiry: experience and story in qualitative research* (first edition). San Francisco: Jossey-Bass

Connell, RW (1985) *Teachers' Work.* Sydney and London: Allen and Unwin

Cooper, P M (2003) Effective white teachers of black children: teaching within a community. *Journal of Teacher Education* 54(5) p413-427

Epstein, C (1972) *Affective Subjects in the Classroom: exploring race, drugs and sex.* Scranton, PA: Intext Educational Publishers

Fullan, M (1993) Why teachers must become change agents. *Journal of Educational Leadership* 50(6) p12-17

Gaine, C (2001) 'If it's not hurting it's not working': teaching teachers about race. *Research Papers in Education* 16(1) p93-113

Gaine, C (2005) *We're All White, Thanks: the persisting myth about 'white' schools.* Stoke on Trent: Trentham Books

Gillborn, D and Youdell, D (2000) *Rationing Education: policy, practice, reform and equity.* Buckingham: Open University Press

Hollway, W (1984) Gender difference and the production of subjectivity. In Henriques, J, Hollway, W, Unwin, C, Venn, C and Walkerdine, V (ed) *Changing the Subject.* London: Methuen

Kehily, M J (2002) *Sexuality, Gender and Schooling: shifting agendas in social learning.* London: Routledge

Knowles, J G (1992) Models of understanding preservice and beginning teachers' biographies: illustrations from case studies. In Goodson, I (ed) *Studying Teachers' Lives.* London: Routledge

Macbeath, J (1998) *Raising Standards – Setting Targets: The Improving School Effectiveness Project – Summary for Secondary Schools.* Edinburgh: The Scottish Office

MacDonald, A (2007) Becoming Chartered Teachers: issues of status, power and identity. *Scottish Affairs* 61 p121-138

Pearce, S (2003) Compiling the white inventory: the practice of whiteness in a British primary school. *Cambridge Journal of Education* 33(2) p273-288

Ras, N (2004) On choosing a theoretical lens in education change research or the road not taken. *Quarterly Journal of Ideology* 26(3/4)

Richardson, R (1990) *Daring to be a Teacher.* Stoke on Trent: Trentham Books

Rudduck, J (1986) A strategy for handling controversial issues in the secondary school. In Wellington, J J (ed) *Controversial Issues in the Curriculum.* Oxford: Basil Blackwell

Russo, P (2004) What does it mean to teach for social justice? It means working to end the cycle of oppression, http://www.oswego.edu/~prusso1/teaching_for_social_justicemain.htm (accessed 17 Feb 2012)

Sachs, J (2003) Teacher activism: mobilising the profession. Paper given at British Educational Research Association Conference, Heriot-Watt University, Edinburgh

Smith, R, Moallem, M and Sherrill, D (1997) How preservice teachers think about cultural diversity: a closer look at factors which influence their beliefs towards equality. *Educational Foundations* 11(2) p41-61

Smyth, J (2004) Social capital and the 'socially just school'. *British Journal of Sociology of Education* 25(1) p19-33

Stone, E (1988) *Black Sheep and Kissing Cousins: how our family stories shape us.* New York: Times Books

Wrigley, T (2000) *The Power to Learn: stories of success in the education of Asian and other bilingual pupils.* Stoke on Trent: Trentham Books

2

Individual teachers making a difference in the classroom and the school

Laura Mitchell

I've never been a great crusader for social justice. I do however feel that it is our consistent approach, the small items, the example we set every day that make the difference. Showing respect for everyone's views, affording all the chance to speak, discussing, showing how to resolve differences. That is what teaching is about. (Secondary teacher of Physics)

This chapter considers how individual teachers, including teaching students, engage in a struggle for social justice in relation to different aspects of their working environment such as education policy, learning resources and the curriculum. It does not deal with the major whole-school changes required to create an ethos of equality across a school, nor does it aim to persuade teachers to become 'crusaders'. Rather, it explores the small changes teachers can bring to their everyday practice and their relationships with pupils which will make an important difference. It presents the experiences and perspectives of three teachers or students through their own voices.

Teachers want the best for their pupils. However, agendas beyond their control often dictate what they will be teaching, how they should teach and how much time they will have to do anything beyond getting through compulsory content. The policy framework promotes inclusion, but is not always clear about how this is to be achieved or how it goes beyond simply providing appropriate individual support so as to address issues of social justice, anti-discrimination and equality.

Teacher engagement and the educational environment
Teacher education

Initial teacher education and CPD provide support for staff trying to wrestle with how to make social justice real in the classroom. This might be by galvanising teachers who feel drained or who lack the confidence and knowledge to tackle issues; by focusing on a theoretical understanding of how inequalities work and therefore how they might be addressed; or more directly by providing strategies for action. Training organisations vary in quality, but the best can drive a major change in thinking across a school or at least provide a few receptive members of staff with the confidence and resources they need to embed new practice in their own classrooms. I say 'a few' because working together can provide the mutual support and collaboration to bring about lasting change in a school, although an isolated individual still has the capacity to make a difference.

Policy and legislation

Legislation has also encouraged teachers to engage with key aspects of equality and social justice in their classrooms and has been a driving force in changing school and local authority policy. When teachers are faced with acts of discrimination or harassment, it is now more likely that they will feel confident to address the matter when they know their actions are supported by policy:

> The change in the legislation with the Equality Act of 2010 has given a massive support to this area of work. The minute [staff] knew they had something to back them, it was crucial. With parents you can now say, 'I'm sorry this is something that is not allowed; it is not legal and is not tolerated'. (Upper primary teacher)

While this heavy-handed approach may be useful on occasions – the visible recording of racist incidents in school may act as a deterrent to racist behaviour for instance – it does not have the educational long-term benefits of embedding principles of social justice into daily practice. It also suggests that social justice is about reacting to injustices rather than proactively engaging with pupils around what social justice means to them.

Personal commitment

Teacher attitude is at the heart of change towards more socially just schooling. Deficit thinking which pathologises minority ethnic, working-class or disabled pupils needs to be unlearned. Pupils' low attainment or lack of engagement is not the consequence of inherent cultural or personal characteristics; it relates to 'the failure of educational systems to respond appropriately to the interaction among teaching, learning and cultures, and diverse students not having the cultural and social capital to successfully negotiate unfamiliar school protocols' (OECD, 2010a). Low aspirations may result from a loss of hope that life can improve, and a teacher's strength of commitment is often the key to an intervention and involvement which can transform a cycle of negativity.

Multicultural learning resources and antiracism

From the early years onwards, it is an important part of education to expand children's experience of the world beyond their child-centred focus and introduce them to the 'other'. Many teachers in nursery and infant classrooms use storybooks, craft activities and so on to bring an awareness of cultural diversity to monocultural classrooms. Similar multicultural approaches can be found in more multi-racial classrooms, which use toys, books, posters and languages to reflect and give recognition to the diversity within the community. In such environments both the children and their families are an additional vital resource.

Typical practices of multicultural education in schools, including days or weeks 'celebrating difference' and projects on Chinese New Year or 'ethnic foods' inserted into the curriculum, have been rightly criticised for their reliance on cultural stereotypes and as inadequate ways of challenging racism (Ladson-Billings, 1998; Gaine, 2005; Gillborn, 2008; Gorski, 2008). However, particularly in the early years, they can be a starting point for exploring issues of racism, discrimination and social inequalities, provided teachers do not get stuck at this level. As Sonia Nieto (2008:28) argues, "being nice' is not enough to combat racism', and the insertion of exotic projects and events into an otherwise mono-cultural Eurocentric curriculum, without seeking to question the validity of this world view, simply privileges white perspectives.

Raising issues of justice through the curriculum
Many resources and strategies have been developed over the years. Puppets or Persona Dolls, alongside approaches such as circle time, can encourage empathy and problem-solving amongst very young children. Further up the primary school, a range of novels, curriculum themes and citizenship education programmes place a focus on global concerns such as globalisation, Fair Trade initiatives, sustainable development, climate control, world poverty, war and unrest, movement of people and questions about refugees and asylum seekers, the United Nations Charter for Children's Rights and so on.

Secondary school subjects vary in their scope for addressing issues of social justice. The emphasis on exam results and the pressure this causes, exacerbated by neoliberal accountability systems, is not always conducive to exploring social justice or collective action which can empower young people to engage with such issues as discrimination or global equality.

Education for citizenship
The development of education for citizenship in the UK's different education systems has provided teachers with the encouragement and opportunity to engage with important real-world issues which might otherwise be neglected. It includes work within specific subjects (eg. Citizenship in England, Modern Studies in Scotland) but also the chance – still too rarely taken up – for whole-school events or interdisciplinary collaboration. (See Paul Vernell's chapter in this book.)

Social justice is integral to citizenship education:

> Education for citizenship equips young people with the knowledge, skills and understanding to play an effective role in public life. Citizenship encourages them to take an interest in topical and controversial issues and to engage in discussion and debate. Pupils learn about their rights, responsibilities, duties and freedoms and about laws, justice and democracy. They learn to take part in decision-making and different forms of action. They play an active role in the life of their schools, neighbourhoods, communities and wider society as active and global citizens. (Department for Education, 2011)

But what about secondary school teachers who do not have opportunities to work on citizenship education programmes, either because it is seen as somebody else's specialism or because the school has not developed provision? Some teachers may find that to embed social justice issues within their teaching subject is fairly straightforward. When teaching about the role of women in society through paintings, or about racism through blues and jazz music, teachers may use the opportunity not just to explore a multicultural range of experiences and knowledge, but also to address values.

On the surface other subjects seem to produce fewer opportunities to raise issues of social justice, but teachers nonetheless succeed in extending beyond their specialist subject:

> Before entering the profession, I was aiming to become a teacher of *Physics* but now, if anyone asks, I am a teacher of *children* ... That subtle change of emphasis altered my entire perspective of my role and although I'm very enthusiastic about my subject, in the end, it's not the subject that's important but the children.

> When you look out for them, there are numerous opportunities in every lesson to talk with individual pupils and find out more about the person behind the jotter – it is very rare indeed to find a child who, when given the chance and the feeling that they are valued, will not want to share something about themselves. (Secondary teacher of Physics)

There are, however, many neglected opportunities even within apparently constrained subjects, since science does not develop in a vacuum: to name just three examples, Galileo defied religious orthodoxy and the power of the Church; Einstein became a refugee when the Nazi party took power in Germany; and Alan Turing, whose genius in code-breaking made a key contribution to Britain's war against fascism, suffered persecution and was driven to suicide only a few years later for his homosexuality.

Building bridges to parents

Taking opportunities to engage with parents is vital to creating an ethos conducive to a socially just school:

> I try and talk to parents quite a lot and make a lot of effort with them and talk about the social pressures that they feel and I think that helps. To talk to the parents of the footballing boys who worry about how to get it right all the time, or the parents of the girls who worry about having the right clothes, and so on. These are the social issues that the kids really worry

about and I try to undercut that early on in discussions with the parents. (Upper primary teacher)

Building positive partnerships with parents and the wider community is high on policy agendas, but is sometimes entered into with an understandable degree of trepidation. When tackling discriminatory behaviour from pupils, teachers can feel that 'giving parents a greater say in the control of schools calls into question the claim to professional autonomy, and perhaps more damagingly exposes the weaknesses of teachers' work in areas where they do not actually have full control or effective solutions (for example, on discipline)' (Connell, 1985:201).

Taking time to get to know parents and discuss their fears and concerns in an open, equal and honest dialogue is not always easy, but both staff and parents ultimately want what is best for the child and from that starting point it is possible to negotiate solutions. What is difficult for the teacher is also difficult for the parent, so making contact with parents, listening to their worries and telling them good news stories about their child in addition to discussing concerns, can help break down some of the barriers.

> The hard-to-reach parents are usually those who are scared of school from their own experiences. What I do with them is I phone them. I make the contact by phone and then physically – I actually physically hold their hand and shake their hand and somehow that can make a difference. (Upper primary teacher)

As Harris and Goodall point out, parents' social status correlates with their ease in liaising with teachers:

> So, certain parents are more likely to engage in learning, while others face certain barriers, influenced by context and culture, which can be wrongly interpreted as resistance or intransigence. Parental engagement is going to be possible with certain groups only if major efforts are made to understand the local community, and if the relationship is perceived to be genuinely two-way. (Harris and Goodall, 2008:286)

The initiative in breaking down barriers has to come from the school, given its symbolic power; even confident parents can feel shut out. Strategies might include taking into account parents' other work or childcare commitments, providing interpreters and arranging informal social occasions where parents can find out about the school.

In a study of school partnerships with minority ethnic parents in the North of England, Crozier and Davies (2007) found that many schools are:

> not sufficiently welcoming to these minority ethnic parents ... to help the parents overcome their own apprehensions about their lack of educational knowledge, levels of English or even how they will be received as 'Asian' and Muslim people. The schools have also failed to address racist abuse towards their children ... therefore ... represent spaces of exclusion; unwelcome spaces where few Bangladeshi and Pakistani parents have a voice. (Crozier and Davies, 2007:311)

Dealing with racism and other forms of discrimination therefore has some immediate benefits for a school: it creates improved learning environments for all the pupils and convinces parents that they can trust the school.

Perspectives

I am always conscious when visiting schools of the homogeneity of the workforce here in Scotland, and often think of Paul Gorski's phrase, 'the luxury of my whiteness' (Gorski, 2000:30). Even in more diverse parts of Britain such as the larger English cities, the teaching profession is still predominantly white (Mills, 2008; Lander, 2011). This poses a number of questions: can the present workforce best understand and meet the needs of minority ethnic pupils and their families, and, if so, how? Will teachers always be able to recognise racism in the school. Whether it is conscious or unconscious? In teaching about discrimination, teachers have to take initiatives and be ready to learn about discrimination alongside pupils.

In one school I visited in the overwhelmingly white Scottish Highlands, a teacher was trying to use aspects of critical pedagogy to explore issues of racism with her lower secondary English class. She had read an essay by Peggy McIntosh (1990) which described how the author identified 'some of the daily effects of white privilege in my life' by drawing up a list of 50 unsought advantages relating to whiteness. The teacher did a similar exercise with her all-white class, followed by a discussion about the experiences of racism they had found in Mildred D. Taylor's *Roll of Thunder, Hear My Cry.*

Follow-up lessons involved biographies of Martin Luther King and Nelson Mandela, and poetry such as Carol Ann Duffy's *Comprehensive* and Benjamin Zephaniah's *What Stephen Lawrence has taught us*. This linked to work in modern studies on equalities, racism and anti racist legislation. Reference was made throughout these lessons to the UN Charter for Children's Rights with which the pupils were familiar from their primary schools.

Such focused use of texts can allow children and teachers to work together to develop a level of empathic understanding. The interdisciplinary nature of this example also helped embed the message, as pupils saw racism from at least two perspectives. Other initiatives can be developed around projects from local or national organisations such as Show Racism the Red Card. However, the impact is considerably enhanced when such learning is extended through the children's school experience, rather than one-off lessons or projects.

Learning to be critical

When visiting a student on an upper primary placement in a large school serving an area of severe poverty and deprivation, I was struck by her ability to embed issues of social justice into her teaching. She took every opportunity to use examples which raised issues such as global poverty, racism or children's rights. The lesson I observed was about World War II propaganda, but this was prepared for by looking at anti-bullying posters, appeals to give blood and the Make Poverty History campaign.

> The children ... discussed the messages behind the posters, one of those being the role of women ... Children fed back their understandings of the need for women to start working since a lot of men were fighting in the war. This led to discussion of gender roles and the changes which occurred during and after the war, encouraging the children to think about how women felt after they'd been able to work and earn their own money then being expected to go back to being housewives. This enabled them to connect the changing roles of women to their own lives. (Third year primary student teacher)

The student drew attention to issues in ways which avoided portraying people as victims; the lessons highlighted their ability to act as change-makers. She took additional opportunities to embed social justice through incidental learning, as well as specifically chosen curricular inputs. For instance, building on children's natural interest in fairness, she engaged pupils in discussion around the World War II topic they were studying:

> We read a chapter of *The Boy in the Striped Pyjamas* and stopped to discuss social justice issues such as Hitler [as dictator of Germany], whether this was fair, [and] if it was fair for Bruno to be saluting and saying 'Heil Hitler' when he didn't know what this meant. During a later school trip a child asked whether all Germans were 'evil'. I asked whether they thought Bruno and his family were all bad which allowed the children to talk about race and nationality. To try and link this to their lives, I asked whether they thought all Scottish people were 'good' and we discussed what this meant. (Third year primary student teacher)

This form of substantive conversation was a part of her everyday teaching approach. She told me she had been initially unsure about doing this as it made her feel vulnerable, but once she started it became a natural part of her practice and she was quickly gaining confidence in finding the right questions to ask:

> I had been thinking about [social justice] quite a lot before starting this placement and I worried about how I would do it and fit it into everything, but once I started thinking about it, it was actually quite easy. By thinking on your feet you can embed issues into almost anything and it relates to the everyday lives of the children. (Third year primary student teacher)

This goes well beyond the basic 'being nice' understanding of some students, and also an understanding of social justice which is limited to *inclusion* that provides personal support to those with barriers to learning. Such inclusion is important, especially with the increasing diversity of needs and abilities in classrooms, but this student demonstrated that a more ambitious approach to social justice also benefits all pupils in terms of learning and classroom ethos. The higher-order thinking skills being developed in relation to social justice helped motivate and engage pupils, strengthened their learning and built their self-esteem and co-operation:

> You can talk about social justice in almost anything. In maths, the children researched on computers the cheapest places to buy things. This made them think about buying products and why you might buy certain things. A lot of children commented that their mums bought smart-price stuff

because it's so cheap. I asked them what they would do if they had lots of money and didn't have to think about the price. This got them talking about the attitudes different social classes may have when doing a basic food shop. (Third year primary student teacher)

Recognition: challenging stereotypes

Other teachers mentioned the importance of being able to think on your feet. One teacher who was trying to address the heterocentric dominance in her class talked about how she had to be thoughtful in her use of language:

Using the word *partner*, and also always saying, 'when you guys choose whoever you end up having a relationship with, whether it be a man or a woman', and it is just gently embedding that kind of message. (Upper primary teacher)

Children did not always react positively to this challenge to their thinking:

Sometimes when I get a screwed-up face, which I sometimes do, I say, 'What's that about? What's going on?' And they say, 'Well we thought X, Y, Z' and you say, 'Really? Well why do you think that? Why do you think that it has to be this way or this way?, and they'll usually say, 'Well because that's what my dad says you have to do'. And then you go, 'OK, but it doesn't have to be that way because we all know that people are quite different. We all have different appearances, we all have different ways of being and different tastes, so why can't we have different sorts of partners and different ways of living and loving?' (Upper primary teacher)

The justice of *recognition* (Young, 1990; Fraser, 1997) is central. Where children are misrecognised due to their background, be it social class, ethnicity, language, disability, sexuality or gender, their engagement with education will be limited. This does not just mean that teachers need to be aware of a child's background, they also need to address the normativity of the homogenous classroom where the dominant culture, such as hegemonic masculinity, prevents children from exploring alternative visions of themselves and the world around them:

Take my class of fairly hard, football-loving primary sevens, who are doing finger knitting right now and are going to sell their wares as part of an enterprise project. That is about challenging kids to be creative and being allowed to like pink and fluffy and encouraging them to express themselves and to be cool doing something that is a bit different. (Upper primary teacher)

The teacher is making a conscious effort to challenge the hegemonic masculinity of some of the boys and does so by appealing to their sense of power within the class, so using their sense of themselves to subvert the very thing that gives them that sense of dominance:

The way I do it is quite sly, in that I take aside the really cool kids in the class, who are beautiful footballers, very keen and very good and I say, 'Guys, what do you think about this as a money-making idea?' You know these phases they have – the bands they wear round their wrists – I say, 'How about if we make our own and start our own phase?' And if you get them on board, then it becomes cool. They get right into it and start weaving and they go 'Look at this!' (Upper primary teacher)

Changing contexts

It is always going to be easier to promote social justice in a school where the ethos and support from other staff demonstrate a strong commitment, but it is still possible for an individual teacher to take action in the classroom, especially if this can be extended to co-operation with one or two colleagues and made visible to the rest of the school. Such action is limited by the constraints of society, but good individual teachers play a role only second to a child's home in influencing their future and they can make a difference.

Debra Hayes and colleagues explore this in their book *Teachers and Schooling: making a difference: productive pedagogies, assessment and performance* (Hayes *et al*, 2006). They recognise the constraints of the social climate beyond the scope of the school and the ways in which schools often reproduce inequalities from one generation to the next. However, they conclude that individual teachers can and do take positive steps to make a difference and go on to develop a framework for understanding good teaching known as *productive pedagogies.*

As the secondary Physics specialist explained, he was able to draw on his own life for examples of moral dilemmas and use them to engage pupils in substantive conversations. These encouraged them to question their actions and what was happening around them:

I spent over 15 years in industry before coming into teaching and ... was presented with the very real moral issues associated with foreign industry and developing nations. I became extremely concerned about the industrial exploitation of resources and people in developing countries. My lessons often draw on these experiences and I try to put the science that I'm teaching into the context of its impact – both positive and negative – on different communities. By encouraging pupils to think about the wider issues and pulling in many cross-curricular ideas, the questions often stimulate some very interesting debates. (Secondary teacher of Physics)

Entering into such conversations with pupils encourages 'sustained dialogue between students, and between teachers and students' (Hayes *et al*, 2006:42). In this case, the teacher not only addresses issues of social justice but makes the jump from specific subject knowledge to contextualising that knowledge and relating it to wider social issues. This is in line with current policy guidance to link subjects to one another and to real life.

In Scotland, *Curriculum for Excellence* opens up opportunities for teachers to develop critical pedagogical approaches which encourage learning about social justice throughout the curriculum. The curriculum is more tightly constrained in England, but social justice is still officially highlighted as important, for example in the new inspection regulations (Ofsted, 2011) – though English politicians and policy-makers are mistaken if they believe that teachers can be bludgeoned into adopting a social justice stance. Teachers have considerable autonomy in choosing whether to address issues of social justice or ignore them, for example whether to gloss over discrimination under the blanket coverage of 'behaviour management' and anti-bullying. Changing the classroom culture is a professional responsibility for teachers, who must learn about individual pupils in the class, and about forms of inequality, how they impact on student learning and how they can be addressed through teaching. Understanding the theories concerning social justice enables teachers to recognise injustices in everyday situations and events, and determine how best to respond by making small changes to their practice. Small changes do make a difference.

References

Connell, RW (1985) *Teachers' Work*. Sydney and London: Allen and Unwin

Crozier, G and Davies, J (2007) Hard to reach parents or hard to reach school? A discussion of home-school relations, with particular reference to Bangladeshi and Pakistani parents. *British Educational Research Journal* 33(3) p295-313

Department for Education (2011) Guidance on Citizenship Education, http://www.education.gov.uk/schools/teachingandlearning/curriculum/secondary/b00199157/citizenship/ks3 (accessed 11 Dec 2011)

Fraser, N (1997) *Justice interruptus: critical reflections on the 'postsocialist' condition*. New York and London: Routledge

Gaine, C (2005) *We're All White, Thanks: the persisting myth about 'white' schools*. Stoke on Trent: Trentham Books

Gillborn, D (2008) *Racism and Education: coincidence or conspiracy?* London: Routledge

Gorski, P (2000) Narrative of whiteness and multicultural education. In Gorski, P, Shin, G and Green, M (ed) *Professional Development Guide for Educators*. United States: National Education Association of the United States

Gorski, P (2008) Good intentions are not enough: a decolonizing intercultural education. *Intercultural Education* 19(6) p515-525

Harris, A and Goodall, J (2008) Do parents know they matter? Engaging all parents in learning. *Educational Research* 50(3) p277-289

Hayes, D, Mills, M, Christie, P and Lingard, B (2006) *Teachers and Schooling Making a Difference: productive pedagogies, assessment and performance*. Crows Nest: Allen and Unwin

Ladson-Billings, G (1998) Just what is Critical Race Theory and what's it doing in a nice field like education? *International Journal of Qualitative Studies in Education* 11(1) p7-24

Lander, V (2011) Race, culture and all that: an exploration of the perspectives of White secondary student teachers about race equality issues in their initial teacher education. *Race, Ethnicity and Education* 14(3) p351-364

McIntosh, P (1990) White privilege: unpacking the invisible knapsack. *Independent School* 49(2) p31-6

Mills, C (2008) Making a difference: moving beyond the superficial treatment of diversity. *Asia-Pacific Journal of Teacher Education* 36(4) p261-275

Nieto, S (2008) Nice is not enough: defining caring for students of colour. In Pollock, M (ed) *Everyday Racism: getting real about race in school*. New York: The New Press

OECD (Organisation for Economic Co-operation and Development) (2010a) *Educating Teachers for Diversity: meeting the challenge*, Paris: OECD Publishing

Ofsted (2011) The framework for school inspection, from January 2012, http://www.ofsted.gov.uk/resources/draft-framework-for-school-inspection-january-2012 (accessed 12 Dec 2011)

Young, I M (1990) *Justice and the Politics of Difference*. Princeton, N J: Princeton University Press

3

Learning about concepts, terminology and theories: from ambiguity to clarity

Shereen Benjamin and Akwugo Emejulu

Introduction

Education is a key site for struggles over equality and justice. From the ways in which educators and policy-makers define 'education', decide who are 'successful learners', determine the content of curricula and configure relationships in classrooms, education is deeply political. It can generate views, perspectives and expectations that foster critique and problematisations of the ways in which we organise our social life. When we say that education is 'political', we mean much more than which political party you vote for, or even which party's education policies you support. We mean that education at all levels is shaped by relations of power, for instance, between policy-makers and practitioners, between teachers and pupils and between headteachers and more junior staff. Within each of these relations of power exist between different social groups, such as women and men, members of different social classes or different ethnic and racial groups. For educational practices to help support learning for democracy, equality and progressive social change, we need to have a firm grasp of differing conceptions of social justice and their implications for teaching, curricula and social relations in schools.

In this chapter we seek to discuss what social justice might signify in relation to teacher education and professional practice. By social justice we mean those ideas and actions that help to create a 'community in which people stand in relations of equality to others' (Anderson, 1999: 289). In other words, social justice is a theory and practice that fosters democratic relations and social solidarity in order to build a society that is based on equality, liberty and respect.

We have organised this chapter in two parts. Firstly, we define what social justice is and discuss key definitions of this concept in political theory. In particular, we explore the way in which social justice is typically conceptualised as *redistribution* (in terms of the fair allocation of income, wealth and resources in a given society) and as *recognition* (in terms of fostering respect and dignity for difference in democratic public life) (Young, 1990, 1997; Fraser, 1997, 2005; Pearce and Paxton, 2005; Lister, 2007; Craig *et al*, 2008).

In the second half of the chapter we consider how social justice can be put into practice in the classroom. We examine how teachers can take socially just ideas forward through the ways in which they relate to their colleagues and pupils in a school-based environment. By considering how we use language to bring certain ideas of (in)equality into our everyday educational lives and the ways in which relationships in the school can be reconstructed to work from locations of egalitarianism, this might help provide concrete ways in which teachers can advance social justice at the community level.

Conceptualising social justice from the position of the least advantaged

Following the political philosopher John Rawls (1971), we think the best way to start conceptualising the idea of social justice is to begin with his famous thought experiment. Imagine you were part of a group seeking to build a new society. What should that society look like? How do you decide on levels of equality and freedom enjoyed by the people of this society? Should these people be democratic citizens or subjects of another system of government? In the social relations of the people in your new society, how concerned should you be about levels of poverty, inequality, discrimination or violence? In our attempts to answer these questions about our new society's organisation, we quickly get steered into broader debates about morality, ethics and the best way of creating a 'good society' in which individuals can flourish.

Rawls argues that the most important way to judge the morality and justice of any society is to consider it from the vantage point of the least advantaged. In order to make decisions about the ethics of the new society we wish to create, Rawls suggests we consider what the best possible society would be if we did not know what our own social position in it would be. So in this new society, you might have significantly less income and wealth than others or you might be a member of a despised minority group. You might also be vulnerable – or assumed by others to be vulnerable – because you have a disability. Being in a position of relative disadvantage may radically change what we think is fair and just. It is these thorny debates about what is fair that form the basis of social justice.

In contemporary debates about what social justice is and how it can be achieved, the starting point usually relates to the practice of liberty, equality and democracy (Young, 1997; Fraser, 2005; Lister, 2008). These three ideas are taken as normative values – they have an intrinsic importance in their own right, since liberty, equality and democracy are the gateway to a life well-lived and fundamental to building a fair society. However, when we look at different groups' social and economic outcomes in relation to these ideas, we see that because of their social positions, some groups appear to have unequal access to the mechanisms which lead to the good life. Here are a few examples that illustrate this point.

Liberty

Compared to their white counterparts, young African-Caribbean and Asian men are far more likely to be stopped and searched by the police (*Guardian*, 2010). Regardless of their class backgrounds or criminal histories, these men are usually prime targets for being stopped, questioned and/or detained. Stop and search can be seen as a self-fulfilling prophecy; because a larger proportion of young black and Asian men are stopped and searched, it is assumed that it is mostly black and Asian men who commit the majority of crimes. This impacts on the liberty of these groups to interact freely in the public spaces of our towns and cities. Associating young black and Asian men with crime might also make it difficult for other groups to *recognise* them as more than just thugs or troublemakers.

Equality

Young women typically outperform their male counterparts in education – they leave school with more qualifications, are more likely to go to university and do better than their male peers in higher education (Scott, 2008). However, women still experience significant labour market discrimination: although they are better qualified they are less likely to earn the same amount as men or be promoted into management and leadership positions. Gender therefore has an important influence on women's equality in the workforce.

Democracy

People living in poverty are less likely to vote or to participate in democratic decision-making about their communities (McKendrick *et al*, 2011). Poverty is not simply about levels of income and wealth, it is also a state of being actively excluded from the levers of power in a given society. One of the main ways in which people living in poverty are excluded from our democracy is through the negative representations of 'the poor' in the media and popular culture and the impact this has on the ability of people with experiences of poverty to gain a voice and respect from other citizens to actively participate in public life (Lister, 2008).

We can see how social justice is primarily concerned with the organisation of 'social arrangements that permit all to participate as peers in social life' (Fraser, 2005:73). Social justice refers to the process by which we reconstruct our social relations to ensure that they are practised on the basis of respect and equality and allow everyone to take part in our democracy. It is therefore important to see social justice as holding both normative and instrumental values. In possessing a value in its own right, social justice can be said to be a *normative* value because a good society in which individuals flourish is one that is socially just. Social justice is also *instrumental* because democracy is strengthened by the achievement of genuine liberty and equality for all citizens.

In contemporary debate, social justice is usually understood as a two-pronged concept relating to the *redistribution* of income, wealth and resources and the *recognition* of difference. We now discuss each of these concepts.

Understanding the redistribution and recognition paradigm

Thinking about social justice as redistribution is the dominant way of considering fairness and probably the most familiar to you. Redistributive justice is concerned with the fairness with which 'the good and bad things in life' are distributed across different social groups (Miller, 1999: 1). Rather than assuming that the current allocation of income, wealth and resources is natural or immutable, redistributive justice forces us to consider how the economic structure of our society – capitalism and social relations under the class system – generates and reproduces significant inequalities and injustices for particular individuals and groups.

From the perspective of redistributive justice, economic privilege and disadvantage are not seen as an individualised phenomenon. The so-called economic winners and losers in a given society are not wholly determined by the actions of individuals, but are the routine outcome of the functions of capitalist development and the operation of social class. For example, some groups are more at risk than others of living on low income or in poverty. Regardless of their educational outcomes, minority ethnic women are more likely than their white counterparts to be living in poverty (Emejulu, 2008). Women are in a similarly precarious financial position in comparison to their male peers (Scott, 2008), especially after separating from their partner or reaching retirement.

What explains the unequal economic outcomes of these diverse groups? Are women and minority ethnic people simply lazy individuals who fail to work hard enough to get ahead in life?

To understand the unjust economic outcomes of some groups, redistributive justice explores how injustice is embedded in a labour market, tax and benefit system and welfare state that systematically disadvantage some groups rather than others. Nancy Fraser (1997:10) argues that economic injustice can be understood in three different ways:

- **exploitation**: individuals and groups can be considered economically exploited when other people disproportionately benefit from their labour. This is usually seen in work that is low-paid, has low status and brings few benefits to the worker

- **marginalisation**: occurs when groups are over concentrated in low-skilled and low-waged work with few opportunities for advancement

■ **deprivation**: individuals and groups can be considered deprived when their work and/or the social protection from the state offers inadequate living standards to lead a dignified life.

Returning to our examples, we can understand how the operation of the labour market results in the economic exploitation and margina-lisation of many minority ethnic groups. Such individuals are either over concentrated in low-skilled, low-waged work or excluded from the labour market altogether because of persistent and systemic labour market discrimination in hiring and promotion (Emejulu, 2008). For women, the combination of sex discrimination in the labour market and the undervaluing of caring responsibilities – deemed to be econo-mically unproductive – concentrates them in the kinds of exploitative and marginal work that lead to deprivation (Scott, 2008; Women's Budget Group, 2010). The unequal economic outcomes of women and minority groups are not a question of their moral failings. Rather, it is our economic system that devalues particular groups and activities and makes it difficult for these groups to afford a decent quality of life.

The central challenge of redistributive justice is focusing on the opera-tion of economic structures and not simply on individual actions. Another important question is: what is the most just way to re-allocate resources? It is beyond the bounds of this chapter to discuss the ways in which justice can be achieved through redistribution. The most common is through the tax and benefit system and the welfare state. A progressive tax system that imposes the strongest tax on the rich and redistributes wealth downwards through a social protection system is one of the most efficient and effective ways of achieving economic jus-tice. By endeavouring to ensure equality of opportunity in life chances through the provision of high-quality education, health and social wel-fare services, such a system can support a more equitable level of fair-ness amongst different groups in society. With the ongoing economic crisis and recent moves to roll back the frontiers of the welfare state, however, we should be alert to attempts to weaken the practice of this form of social justice.

Redistributive justice may be the dominant form of social justice but it certainly is not comprehensive. The various ways in which injustice is manifested are neither adequately captured nor addressed in the language and ideas associated with redistribution. As Iris Marion Young (1990) and Nancy Fraser (1997) note, it can be very difficult to conceptualise justice around ideas that cannot be redistributed such as decision-making, public participation and the nature of social relations. While it makes sense to talk about redistributing wealth, justice encompasses more than income, wealth and class relations.

Over the last twenty years, contemporary social justice theorists have considered new dimensions of social justice and this has led to the idea of justice as recognition. Recognition can be understood as the space that is created and the positive value that is attributed to different ways of being and different interpretations of social life. Recognition is about supporting, respecting and defending *difference* – those identities, cultures and social practices that are not represented by the majority of the public or dominant social norms.

The radical social movements of the 1960s inspired the focus on the recognition of difference. The Civil Rights, women's liberation, gay liberation and disability rights movements were not simply fought on the basis of equal citizenship and economic justice; they were also recognition struggles that sought to undermine the ways in which the dominant culture devalued, disrespected and silenced less powerful groups' cultures and their ways of seeing and understanding the world (Hobson, 2003; Young, 1997).

A focus on justice as recognition asks us to consider the ways in which the representation and interpretation of different ways of being are subjugated to dominant norms and values. Iris Marion Young (1990) argues that injustice as *misrecognition* manifests itself in three different ways:

- **cultural domination**: groups are subjugated when only one way of seeing the world is imposed on them and their perspective is devalued

- **non-recognition**: misrecognition occurs when a group's culture, norms and values are rendered invisible and their perspective is silenced

- **disrespect**: groups are misrecognised when they or their culture are subject to persistent stereotyping and disparaging representations by the dominant culture.

Misrecognition is not necessarily about a group's socio-economic status, it is about the ways in which a minority or less powerful group is represented and portrayed by the majority culture. Returning to an earlier example, living in poverty can be understood as a two-pronged injustice derived from both the unequal distribution of wealth and the misrecognition of difference.

The misrecognition of living in poverty arises in several ways. The current trend of talking about so-called 'benefit scroungers' is a pernicious way of misrecognising people who are living in poverty. In the discourse about 'benefit scroungers' it is assumed that most people who receive benefits are lazy, feckless and unwilling to work. It is also assumed that the benefits system creates a level of 'dependency' that saps the poor of the desire to work.

When we explore the empirical data about living on benefits and consider claimants' attitudes to work, the picture is very different. Firstly, most people who claim benefits are actually working – they receive child benefit, tax credits and housing benefit (McKendrick *et al*, 2011). Secondly, most people who are in receipt of jobseeker's allowance (unemployment insurance) are usually only out of work for short periods of time – notwithstanding the current economic downturn, being unemployed is typically a temporary rather than permanent state for most people. Finally, most people who are unemployed or underemployed do want to work: the problem is a lack of jobs and an absence of affordable childcare that would help people to remain in work (Women's Budget Group, 2010). The misrecognition of people living in poverty is insidious. The assumption that the majority of poor people are benefits cheats disregards the reality presented by the data and completely miscasts those in receipt of benefits. The misrecognition also attaches disrespectful values to people living in poverty. As the discourse of the benefit cheat has gained legitimacy in popular culture, other forms of disrespecting the poor have become acceptable through the discursive use of stereotypes like 'chavs' and 'neds' (Jones, 2010; Connor, 2010). Such misrecognition additionally undermines public confidence in social welfare – which has dire consequences for securing redistributive justice.

The 'elimination of institutional domination and oppression' (Young, 1990:15) is the goal of thinking about and enacting justice as recognition.

This kind of justice practice works to dismantle and interrupt taken-for-granted attitudes and behaviour that perpetuate the misrecognition of different social groups. Focus on recognition is concerned with how we reconstruct our social relations to make them non-oppressive and egalitarian so that different groups have the space and opportunity to articulate their perspectives, live meaningful lives and participate as equals in building a good society where everyone can flourish.

From this brief discussion, we have shown how social justice is a complex idea. The route to simplifying this issue might not be easy or obvious for an interested teacher. We now discuss how these ideas translate into the school and classroom and how socially just practices can be embedded into your everyday teaching life.

Practising social justice in schools

Individual teachers often feel they have little opportunity to challenge social injustice in school, and they can feel overwhelmed by the social inequalities experienced within their school communities. Such a view is understandable. In terms of pupil and student attainment, some patterns of relative success in school-leaving qualifications have stubbornly endured over time, with socio-economic status still a significant determinant of who will do well in school (see eg. Bynner and Joshi, 2002; Raffe *et al*, 2006).

In terms of classroom relationships, research over several decades tells us that boys generally dominate classroom and playground space as well as teacher time (see Clarricoates, 1978; Mac An Ghaill, 1994; Dalley-Trim, 2007). Such evidence can be disempowering: if these patterns have persisted over decades, can we, as individual teachers, really do anything about them? But if we understand classroom action as a consequence of the interplay between macro and micro levels (or between society-wide forces and interpersonal relationships) we begin to see the teacher as capable of making a difference to the promotion of social justice in their own classroom.

What happens in schools and classrooms is often the result of the interplay between the macro and the micro. For instance, the four constituent countries of the UK have their own curricula, which are agreed at national level. The degree of guidance and prescription varies among

41

the four countries, but each holds the principle that all children are entitled to a common curriculum. That curriculum however is mediated by schools, individual teachers and, where relevant, local authorities. Other bodies also play a part in the mediation process: these might include examination boards and publishing companies.

For most teachers, the place where we can make a difference is at the micro-level, in our own teaching and our contributions to school policy. However the teaching we do, and the relationships we have within our school communities, are themselves shaped by macro-level policies and structures. The context for this shaping is difference: how we recognise, value and work with individual and group differences will be crucial to whether we are able to promote social justice in our work and how we will do so.

It is therefore vital to consider the interplay between the macro and micro in terms of redistribution and recognition. In considering redistributive justice, we might think, for instance, about how economic injustices are played out in classrooms and what teachers can do to mitigate them. Obvious examples include funding for extra-curricular activities such as school trips and the provision of spare PE kits or art materials. These may seem straightforward things to think about, but they are often surprisingly difficult to do.

Thinking about how misrecognition is played out in schools – and how teachers might address it – is more complex. As we said earlier, recognition is about restructuring our social relations to make them non-oppressive and egalitarian so that different groups have the space and opportunity to articulate their perspectives, live meaningful lives and participate as equals in building a good society where everyone can flourish.

An important step in the reconstruction of social relations is to be explicit in our thinking about difference. In the 1970s and 1980s the disability movement (a coalition of disabled people fighting oppression and demanding a more equal society on their own terms) coined the term 'social model of disability' (Oliver, 1990). They rejected the idea that disability was caused by disabled people themselves who were in some way defective and needed to be fixed and argued instead that disability is the outcome of a disabling society that constructs barriers to the participation of some of its citizens. The model has been criticised by some for being over-simplistic (see Shakespeare and Watson, 2002). However the notion of a social model and what we might call a 'deficit model' is helpful in thinking about how we might practise justice as recognition in a range of different social groups within our schools and classrooms.

A deficit model of difference sees the source of any problem as being inherent within the individual, and the role of the professional as fixing the defective individual so they become like everyone else. To understand how this works, let us imagine that you hear homophobic abuse being directed towards a studious boy. If your conceptual framework is based on a deficit model of difference, you might think that the boy simply doesn't behave 'boyishly' enough. You might then think that your job is to advise him to spend more time on the football field, as success there would make the homophobic abuse less likely. In this approach, the problem is located with the boy himself, and the solution lies in the need for him to change. You have misrecognised the boy as problematic, made judgements about him based on stereotypical expectations and violated his right to human dignity and respect.

However, if your conceptual framework is based on a social model of difference, the problem would more likely to be seen as homophobia or heterocentrism. Viewed in that way, your job would be to challenge the abuse, consult and possibly review any relevant school policies and educate all pupils about gender stereotyping. In other words, you would consider that the problem lies with society – and it is institutions and structures (in this case, the school) that need to function differently. In your recognition of the boy as a unique, whole human being who fully deserves to be treated with dignity and respect, you would not attempt to impose a dominant group's values upon him.

How we think about difference and inequality thus has an important effect not only on what we do but on whether we make inroads into the difficult task of reconstructing social relationships and address what have been intractable inequalities. In arguing for the importance of how we think about difference and inequality, we are also arguing for the importance of paying attention to language. Earlier in this chapter we introduced Young's (1990) explanation of misrecognition as cultural domination, non-recognition and disrespect. Some forms of language can be used to convey cultural domination. For instance the universal use of BC and AD (Before Christ and *Anno Domini*) rather than the more neutral BCE and CE (Before Common Era and Common Era) are powerful ways of perpetuating the idea that Western thought has a single, unified and Christian history which silences all others.

Some forms of language also convey non-recognition, most often by their avoidance. We may avoid describing someone as Muslim, or disabled, or gay, either because we are scared about causing offence or because we lack confidence about the correct terminology to use. If we are unable to name differences, however, we risk silencing the cultures, norms and values of various groups and individuals.

What should a teacher do to negotiate this potential minefield? In general, so long as you take care over the language you use, remain sensitive to the language used by members of minority groups themselves, and ask where you are unsure, you are unlikely to cause offence.

We have discussed the importance of how you, as a teacher, conceptualise social justice in practice, and how you construct or disrupt misrecognition in the language you use. We now return to the possibilities and limitations of what teachers can do. No one is suggesting that teachers, as a collective or as individuals, have the sole responsibility for producing a more socially just world. Some of the action you take will be whole-school action and will involve talking issues through with other members of the school community. But it is undeniable that the relationships you construct in your classroom are highly contingent on the experiences pupils bring with them, and those experiences themselves are framed by multiple and intersecting inequalities.

Although there are limits to what teachers can do, this does not excuse them from taking action. A large-scale research project in Queensland, Australia (QSLRS, 2001) asked the question 'what can schools realistically do to address social justice?' The project looked at practices in 24 schools, concentrating on those where the attainment of all pupils was high, including the attainment of pupils from groups that, according to research, tend to do less well.

The study found that classrooms characterised by four dimensions – intellectual quality, connectedness, a supportive classroom environment and working with and valuing difference – 'can make *a* difference as one component part of a social justice project in education' (Hayes *et al*, 2006:31, emphasis in original). In other words, whilst the researchers did not believe that schools and teachers on their own can solve all social injustices, they argued that some patterns of inequalities can be disrupted and challenged in the quest for more egalitarian patterns of distribution and recognition. For the QSLRS team, such disruptions happened in the daily teaching practices of individual teachers, who framed the practices by both challenge and support and by respect for individual and group differences.

Summary

This chapter has introduced some of the foundational ideas related to social justice and discussed how the theories of social justice could be put into practice in a classroom environment. We began by grounding our discussion of social justice in Rawls's (1971) principle of evaluating the justice of any society through the perspective of the least advantaged. Understanding how the most vulnerable and least powerful in society experience everyday life is an important starting point for conceptualising what social justice might mean.

We moved on to discuss social justice as both redistribution and recognition. Redistributive justice is primarily concerned with the fairness with which income, wealth and resources are allocated to different social groups. Justice as recognition focuses on how minority groups are represented within the dominant social norms and what spaces can be created for the practice of difference. We argued that to foster genuine democracy in which everyone can participate regardless of background or circumstance, educational practitioners must have a clear understanding of social justice.

We then considered how social justice might be practised in schools. We argued that to make sense of social justice teachers could think about it in terms of macro and micro spaces for practice. At the macro-level, for example educational policy-making, individual teachers can realistically have only a limited impact. However, in the micro-level spaces of schools and classrooms, teachers can make a real difference. Part of making a difference is about creating a culture between your fellow teachers and pupils based on the values of equality, dignity and respect. Having an impact is about supporting a social model, meaning that we seek not to simply individualise pupils' social problems but to see them in a broader context and seek remedies that change the quality of our relationships rather than trying to 'fix' a defective individual.

The ideas of social justice are complex and can seem far removed from day-to-day classroom practice. The more you work with them, however, and try to use them to explain the daily dilemmas with which you are faced as a teacher, the more sense they will make, and the more useful they will be as ways of understanding and developing your practice. As an educational practitioner, it is important to see social justice as an intentional act to help bring a better and more equal world into being. We hope this book will help you in your struggles for equality, justice and democracy.

References

Anderson, E (1999) What is the point of equality? *Ethics* 109(2) p287-337

Bynner, J and Joshi, H (2002) Equality and opportunity in education: evidence from the 1958 and 1970 birth cohort studies. *Oxford Review of Education* 28(4) p405-425

Clarricoates, K (1978) Dinosaurs in the classroom – a re-examination of some aspects of hidden curriculum in primary schools. *Women's Studies International Quarterly* 1 p353-364

Connor, S (2010) The myth of community? *Concept: The Journal of Contemporary Community Education Practice Theory* 1(3)

Craig, G, Burchardt, T and Gordon, D (ed) (2008) *Social Justice and Public Policy: seeking fairness in diverse societies.* Bristol: Policy Press

Dalley-Trim, L (2007) The boys present ... hegemonic masculinity: a performance in multiple acts. *Gender and Education* 19(2) p199-218

Emejulu, A (2008) The intersection of ethnicity, poverty and wealth. In Ridge, T and Wright, S (ed) *Understanding Inequality, Poverty and Wealth.* Bristol: Policy Press

Fraser, N (1997) *Justice interruptus: critical reflections on the 'postsocialist' condition.* New York and London: Routledge

Fraser, N (2005) Reframing justice in a globalizing world. *New Left Review* 36 p69-88

The Guardian (2010) Black people are 26 times more likely than whites to face stop and search. 17 October 2010 (accessed from the internet 19 Nov 2011)

Hayes, D, Mills, M, Christie, P and Lingard, B (2006) *Teachers and Schooling Making a Difference: productive pedagogies, assessment and performance.* Crows Nest: Allen and Unwin

Hobson, B (ed) (2003) *Recognition Struggles and Social Movements: contested identities, agency and power.* Cambridge: Cambridge University Press

Lister, R (2007) Social justice: meanings and politics. *Benefits* 15(2) p113-125

Lister, R (2008) Recognition and voice: the challenge for social justice. In Craig, G, Burchardt, T and Gordon, D (eds) (2008) *Social Justice and Public Policy: seeking fairness in diverse societies.* Bristol: Policy Press

Mac An Ghaill, M (1994) *The Making of Men: masculinities, sexualities and schooling.* Buckingham: Open University Press.

McKendrick, JH, Mooney, G, Dickie, J and Kelly, P (ed) (2011) *Poverty in Scotland 2011: towards a more equal Scotland?* Glasgow: Child Poverty Action Group

Miller, D (1999) *Principles of Social Justice.* Cambridge, MA: Harvard University Press

Oliver, M (1990) *The Politics of Disablement.* Basingstoke: Macmillan

Pearce, N and Paxton, W (ed) (2005) *Social Justice: building a fairer Britain.* London: Politico's

Queensland School Reform Longitudinal Study (QSRLS) (2001) Research report submitted to Education Queensland by the School of Education, University of Queensland. State of Queensland: Brisbane

Raffe, D, Croxford, L, Ianelli, C, Shapira, M and Howieson, C (2006) *Social-Class Inequalities in England and Scotland.* University of Edinburgh, Centre for Educational Sociology, Special CES Briefing No. 40

Rawls, J (1971) *A Theory of Justice.* Cambridge, MA: Harvard University Press

Scott, G (2008) Gender, poverty and wealth. In Ridge, T and Wright, S (ed) Understanding Inequality, *Poverty and Wealth.* Bristol: Policy Press

Shakespeare, T and Watson, N (2002) The social model of disability: an outdated ideology? *Research in Social Science and Disability* 2 p9-28

Women's Budget Group (2010) *The Impact on Women of the Coalition Spending Review 2010,* http://www.wbg.org.uk/RRB_Reports_4_1653541019.pdf (accessed 22 Nov 2011)

Young, I M (1990) *Justice and the Politics of Difference.* Princeton, NJ: Princeton University Press

Young, I M (1997) Difference as a resource for democratic communication. In Bonham, J and Rehg, W (eds) *Deliberative Democracy: essays on reason and politics.* Cambridge, MA: MIT Press

4

Resolving dilemmas and improving practice in the early career of teaching

Helen Knowles

'*Yorkie: it's not for girls!*' What do you think of when you see this advert? For me it immediately brings to mind the traditional masculine qualities of toughness, physical strength and hiding emotions, placed in opposition to the traditionally feminine qualities of emotion and physical weakness. It says that women are not man enough to eat this chocolate bar. It plays on the assumption that women and men are the opposite of one another. It is this assumption that I want to explore further, reflecting on my own life to look at how social justice has become important to me through my unique past experiences. I then consider how I developed this interest in the classroom.

I am a primary teacher in Scotland and have taught in various schools during my BEd placements, my probation year and nearly four subsequent years in different schools. I teach part-time through choice, currently as a job-share.

My experiences of gender have been quite wide-ranging. My dad went out to work and my mum stayed at home to look after us, though she made it clear that she found this 'old-fashioned'. I was never dressed in gendered colours or given gendered toys to play with and preferred books, tractors and Lego, but the important thing for me was that I was allowed to pursue the activities I wanted to. As a keen reader I was always aware of children's books that presented stereotypical views of gender and I read numerous such books, including *The Famous Five* and many fairytales. I really enjoyed them but found the roles they opened up to men and women very traditional; as a family we often enjoyed a laugh about it. I also read a lot of feminist stories though I wasn't explicitly aware of this quality at the time. I simply knew that different authors presented different views of reality and that I agreed with some and not with others.

My experience of 'race' was quite different. I grew up in a rural part of Scotland and hardly ever met anyone of different ethnicity except in books and on TV. I remember my sister thinking that every black man she saw was Linford Christie. At high school I was in a relationship with a boy who was mixed race and I remember being excited by this new experience. My parents brought me up to see everyone as human and no different to myself. I remember hearing racist and homophobic comments throughout my childhood but I always had the inner confidence to know that I didn't agree with them.

I have grown up in a racist, sexist, homophobic society where hegemonic masculinity is routinely conveyed through public media. Homophobic ridicule is commonplace on television and often defended as a 'bit of fun'. I do not believe that a person can be unbiased which is why I deemed it important to explore my past. I am a product of the millions of interactions I have had with other people, texts and the media throughout my life. This complex set of discursive practices has shaped my unique identity and placed me differently to every other person. I have always been self-critical and found it difficult at first to accept that I have certain assumptions and prejudices, but this confrontation with myself has been important. Until we can become aware of our own prejudices we can never begin to help children work beyond theirs. We must accept that we do not have an impartial view of the world.

To give one example, I had assumed that anybody who got into trouble with the police must be the product of bad parenting. I realised this didn't hold true when I met a friend's brother. Both were brought up in a stable and caring family, but one joined the police force and the other went off the rails. The realisation that not everything can be put down to parenting helps me stay open-minded about the parents of the children in my class.

We need more men in teaching, don't we?

Gender has always fascinated me. I have an overwhelming sense of what is fair and gender always stood out as being particularly unjust. As a keen footballer at school I always found it unfair that women's football was primarily amateur when men's professional football was much more in the public realm. The fact that my sister and I played football was some-times met with either disbelief or a metaphorical pat on the head for having a go. I even had derogatory comments made about my sexuality. From the media I learned that men are paid more than women in some sectors. I studied history to the age of 18 and did a lot of work on the Suffragettes. I was fascinated by the changing role of women.

I was once in a relationship with a farmer's son and was amazed at the limited agency women had in farming circles despite often doing a lot of the physical work. Though I loved the romantic notion of life as a farmer's wife, I knew it went against everything I believed in. There were some incredibly strong discourses at play within his family and amongst his family friends. One asked what my father did for a living as he wanted to know if I was 'suitable'. The revelation that my parents were English was met with jovial gasps and a shaking of heads.

I never had a male primary teacher and was aware that I was entering a predominantly female profession. During voluntary work in schools prior to starting my BEd, the general consensus in staffrooms was that boys needed male teachers as role models. This always seemed illogical to me and I couldn't understand why it was so widely accepted. Surely what matters most is whether your teacher is effective and enthusiastic, not whether they are male or female? A male teacher will only be a role model if he is capable of being so, not just because he is male.

I was also intrigued by the widespread idea of boys' underachievement which has since become widely accepted. I was told in lectures that girls were better than boys at reading and the way to help the boys was to pro-vide more exposure to non-fiction texts. I learned that girls were better at concentrating so boys required a variety of teaching techniques in order to keep them interested. I read books that spoke about brain-based gender differences, and said that teaching should be modified to be more 'boy-friendly' (Gurian, 2003:28). I started to see evidence to sup-port this, failing to notice the overlaps between boys and girls.

My mum also works in a school and had found these approaches effective. She put this down to supposed brain-based differences, which were well known, often reported in the media and discussed by education experts and practising teachers alike. It all made sense. I was surrounded by a belief that the teaching profession saw to be true and I came to believe in its truth also. What worries me is how unaware I was that this was an opinion or belief I held, and one which didn't sit comfortably with my well-established views on gender. Then came the Year 4 gender elective.

Burping boys

When I started the set reading it felt as if I had discovered the missing piece of the puzzle. In poststructural terms gender is relational and fluid; it is performed and developed in relation to others, not fixed and related to physical sex (Davies, 2003:13). My friend's story sums this up perfectly. When her small son burped everyone laughed and this reward encouraged him to do it again. His behaviour was accepted by those around him and continually rewarded. With her daughter, however, the reaction was very different. Nobody laughed when she burped; instead they made sure she excused herself. The reaction gave her a very different message: it told her in no uncertain terms that burping was not acceptable behaviour for girls. The same behaviour is read differently in girls and boys because of the way they are placed by patriarchy (Walkerdine and Lucey, 1989:131). Children are confronted with the gender dichotomy as soon as they are brought into the world. They are given different toys to play with and different behaviour is expected of them and rewarded (Browne and France, 1985:147; Thorne, 1993:2). So they grow up to perform their gender in a culturally acceptable way.

Being aware that gender is socially constructed is really important in class. You might see teachers managing boys' behaviour differently and appealing to the discourse that 'boys will be boys' but as Davies (2003: xii) says, 'by basing our interactions with children on the presumption that they are in some unitary and bipolar sense male or female, we teach them the discursive practices through which they can constitute themselves in that way.'

These studies gave me both a lasting focus on gender and an understanding of how class and ethnicity intersect with it to create a complex network of differences.

A key part of my attitude towards challenging social justice issues comes from the network of support I have. I get my confidence to challenge accepted wisdom from knowing that I have support from my family, friends and a group of like-minded teachers and former tutors from university. Being aware that there are others who believe the same things I do allows me to do this. You don't need to challenge in an aggressive way but can simply involve yourself in the conversation and put your point of view across.

In the real world

When I initially thought about writing this chapter I was unsure as to what I had actually managed to achieve in school. I know that in my personal life I am very vigilant about social justice and can recall many times when I have challenged and questioned practices, views and issues. What I found hard to ascertain was the difference I had made to the children in my class. I felt as if the everyday challenges of teaching, particularly in my probation year, had taken the focus away from what I had found so important at university.

Once I started to discuss it with my family and began to work on some mind maps, however, I realised there were many occasions when I had used a classroom incident as the basis for discussion and learning. I hadn't done anything community-based or outwardly revolutionary. I hadn't piloted a school-wide project on social justice – I had barely stayed in a school long enough to get my teeth into anything more than the day-to-day running of my classroom – but I realised that the classroom was where I had been making a difference. I started to note down all the times when issues relating to social justice had come up and how many interesting discussions I had had with my classes.

In the next section I expand on a few incidents to show how discussing issues of social justice can be an everyday part of learning and teaching. I draw on examples from all the schools I have worked in – schools in different council areas and with classes from P1 (5-year-olds) to P7 (11-year-olds). The names have been changed to protect privacy.

The first discussion came when a seemingly throw-away comment provoked a class discussion on gender and advertising. This allowed the children to start thinking about alternative roles that they could occupy as girls or boys.

'I don't want pink paper!'

I was doing an RE lesson with a Primary 2 class and one of the activities required a blank piece of paper. As the office had over-ordered certain colours of photocopier paper, teachers had to use pink paper instead of white until it ran out. I had nearly finished handing each sheet out when Terry looked at it in disgust and said, 'I don't want pink paper'. The conversation went something like this:

> Terry: I don't want pink paper
>
> Me: Oh, why not?
>
> T: Because pink paper is for girls
>
> M: I see. What makes you think that?
>
> T: Because all pink stuff is for girls
>
> M: What kinds of things do you mean?
>
> T: Like tents and bikes with glitter on them
>
> M: What colour of paper would you like?
>
> T: Blue (looks to Jason)

At this point some of Terry's friends and a few boys from a different group started to complain about the colour of their paper. Terry looked smug and sat back, allowing the others to carry on the argument on his behalf.

Let's look more closely at what Terry is doing here. He refuses to take a pink piece of paper because he is a boy and he believes that pink is not for boys. He gives the reason that pink is for girls and so places himself as opposite to girls. As I mentioned before, the behaviour expected of a good boy is different from that of a good girl. Furthermore, the idea of a good girl and a good boy are set up as opposing ideas: as a binary (Trousdale and McMillan, 2003:2). The binary is the foundation for the social construction of masculinity and femininity and why the Yorkie advert is worded in such a way: as it is assumed that being biologically male or female dictates the characteristics of a male or female, it is also believed that the sex of a person dictates their personality. This is why a person's biological sex is often expressed as the 'natural' way for them to be (Weedon, 1997:94).

Connell (1995:77) defines hegemonic masculinity as:

> the configuration of gender practice which embodies the currently accepted answer to the problem of the legitimacy of patriarchy, which guarantees (or is taken to guarantee) the dominant position of men and the subordination of women.

It is not only women who are subordinated but also 'inferior' males: those who are not tough, unfeeling, white, heterosexual, provider, father (but not carer) and so on.

The 'opposition' of the superior male to the 'others' (see Paechter, 1998: 8) is constructed within hegemonic male discourse, with those associated with the male superior to those associated with the female. Post-structuralism allows us to make visible this binary assumption as discursively constructed and therefore not 'real' (Davies, 1997:13). If a girl performs the same behaviour as a boy, it will not carry the same meaning since it will be judged within the discourse of hegemonic masculinity and in the context of male or female norms. A girl who displays independence might therefore be called a 'right madam' (Walkerdine and Lucey, 1989:201).

If children perform gender according to their sex, the play that is expected of boys and girls is different. As a consequence, boys and girls play separately, and a girl will not want to partake in the violent play of the boys because it is not the type of behaviour that she 'should' be performing (Skattebol, 2006:516).

Jordan (1995:75, quoted in Holland, 2003:20) comments that 'boys have adopted a definition of masculinity in which the subordinate term is the behaviour of females, [and] that being male is primarily doing things that cannot and should not be done by women.' Terry does not want pink because it would make him the opposite and inferior of a boy: a girl. Men are encouraged to eat a Yorkie for the same reason. As Terry is the hegemonic male, his friends must also re-assert their maleness to get back on side and avoid social isolation. Their behaviour has been highlighted as different and they now need to decide how to reposition themselves within the social group. This is hegemonic masculinity in action.

It was at this point that I decided to temporarily abandon the RE lesson and explore the issue of the pink paper a bit further. I stopped the children and asked them which things they thought were for girls and which were for boys. Their answers did not surprise me: on the girls' list were dolls and on the boys' list were guns. Computers were on both lists but the games were quite different; boys cited adventure, war and shooting games while the girls mentioned games that were educational and family-orientated. I then asked the children why they thought these things were for girls or boys. Immediately they started to talk about television. Adverts for pink tents and bikes with glitter and tassels on them had featured girls while Ben 10 adverts had featured boys.

We looked at adverts from the Argos catalogue and I asked them to think about how the adverts were made. We discussed how this was no different to the children drawing a poster: someone decided on the content of the advert and they chose to show lots of girls with the pink bike in the hope that lots of girls would want one.

Whilst these were difficult concepts for young children, opening up this discussion allowed them to see that there are ways of looking at the world besides the most obvious one presented to them (Davies, 2003: 49). It may never have crossed their minds that boys could wear pink, for example, if their mum has a lot of pink clothes and their dad has none.

The lesson reminded me of my BEd dissertation, in which I wrote a poststructural analysis of two children's readings of *The Paper Bag Princess* (Munsch, 2003). It is a story about Elizabeth, an agentic Princess who pursues a dragon, tricks him into saving Prince Ronald, and then decides not to marry him because he is rather rude about her appearance. (She wears a paper bag for most of the book as the dragon burnt all her clothes along with her castle). Inspired by Davies (2003:62), I read it to two 5 year-olds in P1, Mark and Lucy, who could not accept many of the things that happened in the story, including Elizabeth's decision not to get married. They retold the story to fit the traditional fairytale discourse where women are beautiful, often suffer in silence, and are chosen by the prince to live happily ever after. In this discourse, female characters never make their own choice with regards to marriage but always accept the male character's decision instead (Parsons, 2004:137).

Mark's and Lucy's behaviour in the playground was also strongly differentiated, and gendered objects had very definite meanings for them. Mark talked a lot about clothes. He often seemed to be thinking out loud, saying one thing and then contradicting himself. He told me that boys can't wear heels because they'd look like girls. When I asked if there was anything else boys couldn't do, he said they couldn't have long hair. He soon corrected himself, however, as he remembered that quite a few boys in *High School Musical* had long hair.

It was interesting to observe how this was an unquestionable truth for Mark because he had seen it on the big screen. He also talked about boys wearing pink and he said that Ronald in the story could wear pink but not a pink dress or a pink wig; a pink wig would make him look like a girl because Stephanie from *LazyTown* has pink hair. In fact, Stephanie not only has a pink wig, she has a completely pink outfit. Her character is often helpless and fearful and is always saved by Sportacus, a fit and active male superhero who dresses completely in blue and saves the day. So when Mark thinks of pink wigs, he is actually thinking of the whole package.

In the same way, Terry and his friends have seen so much to reinforce the idea that pink is for girls that they can't see past this. The class discussion did not have immediately visible consequences. My P2s didn't transform before my eyes into confident individuals free from gendered clothing, toys and ideas. Terry did not turn up the next day in pink trousers, proud of his new identity. It may take years for the effects of discussions like these to manifest themselves and I certainly don't ever expect to see them. What is important is that I opened up a discursive space which gave the children a chance to see things a little differently. The more this happens, the more children will start to question what they see on television and begin to look beyond the version of reality so often presented to them.

Even in a class of 6-year-olds it is possible to get children to look at literacy critically. In the next section I look at a more structured approach to critical literacy in the classroom.

Only Shreddies are knitted by Nanas

I did a whole term of work with a P7 class (11-year-olds) in which we retold fairytales from different points of view. We began by retelling *Little Red Riding Hood* as a group and it quickly became apparent that children had encountered different versions, orally and on television. This opened up nicely into a discussion about how different stories convey different points of view. We spent time retelling the story in different ways, through writing and drama, using different genres and always focusing on one character's point of view. The big personalities of the class quickly established themselves and various children became the big bad wolf or the heroic woodcutter.

The children then made up the missing parts of the story, including how the woodcutter came to be in the woods and what made him burst into Granny's house. I really wanted them to explore how each character viewed what happened differently. Each child had a separate opinion about the same event and saw their own part in it differently. Following this the children wrote their own version of Red Riding Hood from the point of view of one of the characters. We followed that exercise by watching the film *Hoodwinked* which, while still playing to some stereotypes, shows all the characters in a totally different light. The film also gives alternative versions of the story from each point of view so the assumed motives for the characters' actions are subverted.

Granny is a character that the children enjoyed playing and found the easiest to portray, so I decided to explore this character further. The children had presented her stereotypically: bent over, gossiping with her friends, squeaky-voiced and with no teeth, so I asked them where they got their idea of the stereotypical Granny from. They found this a really difficult question but were eventually able to identify what had shaped their ideas of Granny.

The advert where Nanas knit Shreddies came up, which prompted a lot of discussion about other Granny characters on television. The children also spoke about stories they had read when we talked about the character traits of this idea of Granny. They said she is kind, old, bent over, wears skirts and tights and cardigans, likes baking, has false teeth, looks after everyone and is vulnerable and ill. I then got the children to think about the older people they knew and asked if they fitted this mould. Some of them did but most of them didn't and they soon picked out lots of other attributes that a Granny could have.

Whilst focusing on Granny was related to gender and age, these sessions were more concerned with challenging the fairytale genre generally and opening the children's minds to the possibility of seeing the world in different ways. It also allowed the children to see these stereotypes for what they are and to begin to understand the process of how they came to think these things. As Trousdale and McMillan (2003:3) comment, 'the complex of societal influences, including television, movies, advertisements, magazines, and popular music ... together send strong messages of gender norms and ideals.' With the same message being conveyed in many different ways, this discourse becomes so dominant it seems 'natural' that things are this way. This constructs what Davies (1997:9) calls a 'regime of truth' within which individuals take up positions.

Ursula LeGuin (quoted in Baker, 2006:246) talks about how tradition is so embedded in you that it is hard to subvert it: it is 'older and bigger and wiser than you are. It frames your thinking and puts winged words in your mouth.' Since fairytales present these subject positions and make them available to children (Parsons, 2004:136), working on them helps children to see the gender roles conveyed in these stories as points of view rather than the truth. It also opens up the discursive space to allow girls and boys to be free from the unfavourable character traits that are desired by these discourses including fragility and domesticity in girls and aggression and insensitivity in boys (Davies, 2003:xi). This can provide an opening in which issues related to homosexuality and homophobia can be challenged.

Two strong boys

When the janitor came into my P3 class (7-year-olds) and asked for two strong boys to help him to move some tables, I saw an opportunity to open up a discussion about the discourse of the strong male and weak female. I asked all the children who would like to help and sent two who put up their hands. They happened to be a girl and a boy. I then opened up a class discussion firstly about physical strength and then about other kinds of strength like confidence. We concluded that not all boys were strong and not all girls were weak – which proved to be another small step in opening up what Benjamin calls counter-discursive positionings (2001:43).

Educating about differences

I also want the children in my class to be aware of difference, to accept it and to value difference in other people. I do a lot of discussion, particularly when I first meet the class, about family structures and backgrounds. The children learn about different family structures and discover that they all have different circumstances at home. This sets the tone for the rest of the year and creates a more open space for the children's differences to be discussed.

In recent years a difference-blind approach has become commonplace, whether it is related to race, class or gender (Gaine, 2005:21). This is neither a helpful nor a respectful approach to take. Accepting difference allows discursive space to open up. I don't want all the children to be the same; I want them to accept each other for who they are.

I talk a lot about my own experiences of school too. I struggled with Maths as a child and talking to the children about this allows them to recognise that everyone has different strengths and weaknesses and there are different ways of being successful. If difference is accepted in contexts that children are familiar with, it ought to help them accept difference in other ways.

Summary

As a new teacher you will come across many challenges and it will take you some time to adjust to your new job and all the demands it will make of you. What I hope I have shown in this chapter is that you can challenge issues of social justice every day just by having an awareness of them. This awareness will come from confronting your own assumptions and accepting that you do not have an impartial view of the world. You are then in a position to encourage the children to do the same.

It is easier to teach around generalised issues in the upper school, but don't underestimate the depth of thinking younger children can engage in. Don't be afraid to make mistakes. Take opportunities to discuss discourses when they arise and, most importantly, don't expect instant measurable results. They will probably not show in attainment levels at the end of the year and you may never see these discursive spaces open up at any other time, but what is important is that you facilitate the children's development whenever you can.

We need to give children more space to be themselves. We want young people to have a real choice about how they live their lives.

References

Baker, D (2006) What we found on our journey through fantasy land. *Children's Literature in Education* 37(3) p237-251

Benjamin, S (2001) Challenging masculinities: disability and achievement in testing times. *Gender and Education* 13(1) p39-55

Browne, N and France, P (1985) 'Only cissies wear dresses': a look at sexist talk in the nursery. In Weiner, G (ed) *Just a Bunch of Girls*. Milton Keynes: Open University Press

Connell, R W (1995) *Masculinities*. Cambridge: Polity

Davies, B (1997) Constructing and deconstructing masculinities through critical literacy. *Gender and Education* 9(1) p9-30

Davies, B (2003) *Frogs and Snails and Feminist Tales: preschool children and gender*. New Jersey: Hampton Press

Gaine, C (2005) *We're All White, Thanks: the persisting myth about 'white' schools*. Stoke on Trent: Trentham Books

Gurian, M (2003) *Boys and Girls Learn Differently*. San Francisco: John Wiley and Sons

Holland, P (2003) *We Don't Play with Guns Here: war, weapon and superhero play in the early years*. Berkshire and New York: Open University Press

Munsch, R (2003) *The Paper Bag Princess*. London: Hippo Scholastic

Paechter, C (1998) *Educating the Other: gender, power and schooling*. London: Falmer Press

Parsons, L (2004) Ella evolving: Cinderella stories and the construction of gender-appropriate behaviour. *Children's Literature in Education* 35(2) p135-154

Skattebol, J (2006) Playing boys: the body, identity and belonging in the early years. *Gender and Education* 18(5) p507-522

Thorne, B (1993) *Gender Play: girls and boys in school*. Buckingham: Open University Press

Trousdale, A and McMillan, S (2003) 'Cinderella was a wuss': a young girl's responses to feminist and patriarchal folktales. *Children's Literature in Education* 34(1) p1-28

Walkerdine, V and Lucey, H (1989) *Democracy in the Kitchen*. London: Virago

Weedon, C (1997) *Feminist Practice and Poststructuralist Theory* (2nd edn) Oxford: Blackwell

Section 2
Learning from school and classroom situations

5

Using critical literacy to 'do' gender

Lynne Pratt and Yvonne Foley

Teacher: So do you think that Lady Macbeth has no voice, is silenced then?

Pupil: No, but she's like my mum. She's only got a voice inside the castle. It's Macbeth who really gets to do what he wants. In the end, he's the one with the power. He tells her to shut up and go away. And she does. She kills herself. (Student teacher and S3 pupil in observed lesson, 2010)

In this chapter we describe how we developed our own practice as teacher educators in relation to developing student teachers' understanding of ways in which social justice teaching might be part of lesson planning and delivery. We used critical literacy theories as pedagogy for helping students to structure their thinking and teaching in this area. We focused our teaching on gender but we believe that we could use the same approach to address any area of social justice. Our own practice was enriched and informed by student thinking and we hope that this chapter shows this mutuality.

> How important it is [for teachers] to provide children with tools to investigate their world and the texts which make up that world. (BEd student teacher at Moray House School of Education)

This email comment followed a teaching session with BEd students in our university. Like most student teachers we have encountered, this student is committed to the necessity and desirability of exploring social justice issues and challenging school and classroom discourses of inequality. Her mention of the 'tools' with which teachers might empower children and young people, and that whole notion of how to do it in practice, is a common and reasonable concern of student teachers. Her comment, and others like it, have sensitised us to the needs of student teachers to have a structure to inform their thinking about teaching social justice issues and also the need for teacher educators to develop the positive dispositions of student teachers towards teaching in practice.

Our practice has been informed by our shared interests in the possibility of using critical literacy theories as a way to provide a structure for student teachers to move from a general feeling of social justice being a good thing to social justice being an inherent part of classroom practice.

Our focus is on exploring critical literacy in relation to investigating gender with student teachers and their further use of it as classroom pedagogy. We have selected gender as the teaching focus because texts which inform our understanding of masculinities and femininities are all around us. Our understandings of gender are further complicated by elements of class, power and race, which inform the way gender is constructed in different contexts, including classrooms. Student teachers themselves negotiate discourses in their new professional lives which are gendered. One student teacher, for example, was told to be 'more manly' in the classroom.

Children and young people are equally subject to similar and different texts – be it Barbie to Beyonce and Bieber; or whose toy Lego is meant to be; or to the overwhelming pinkness of the girls' aisle in major toy shops and the shelf of green books for boys in bookshop chains ... the list is endless. For experienced teachers, tackling gender in the classroom can seem extremely difficult; for student teachers and newly qualified teachers (NQTs), it is very risky teaching. However, children and young people need their teachers to take these risks and to challenge some of the limiting discourses of the classroom and the playground.

About critical literacy

Critical literacy is, we believe, a valuable classroom pedagogy. It is particularly useful in situations where thinking can be boundaried, where belief systems seem difficult to challenge and where learning is impeded because it is contextually defined (Luke in Muspratt *et al*, 1997). As theory, critical literacy emerged from Freire's (1970) field practice and as a tool for democratic education. What better place to use it than in the twenty-first century classroom where learner and teacher may encounter rigid or limited ideologies and beliefs about such areas as gender, ethnicity, class and sexuality?

Accordingly, the following section elaborates on some of the key concepts from critical literacy theory. We considered these ideas to be useful to classroom teachers and we drew on them to help student teachers consider how they can be used to inform their planning.

Text

Critical literacy defines text as an item which carries meaning. Text can be written or an image or a combination of both (eg. picture books); it can be a moving image or it can be spoken; it can be digitally communicated or on paper. A spoken text might be a speech, a conversation or an utterance. A text in the history classroom might be an object – a gas mask from World War II perhaps. In Design and Technology, pupils might 'read' the design of a chair. Texts do not have to carry a high cultural value to be worthy of investigation, so Shakespeare and an advert for Barbie can be subject to the same decoding and analytical processes.

If we think about text in this way, consider all the texts we are bombarded with from the moment we wake in the mornings to the point when we close our eyes at night: the radio news, the cereal packet, the text messages, the diary list, the shopping list, etc. This leads us to think about the texts – the same and different – that young learners are subject to and manipulated by. It is therefore important to learn how to deconstruct and understand text and the often implicit ways in which the discourse of power is negotiated within them.

Power

Critical literacy recognises that texts are always about power. The beginning of *Othello*, for instance, is a complex discourse on power. Othello has power because of his military prowess and his personal bravery; his friendship with the ruler of the city; his ability to inspire love in Desdemona and his skill as an orator. His power is challenged by others because he is black and the language used to diminish him is the language human beings often use to diminish others: Othello is compared to animals – 'a black ram is tupping your white ewe' describes the marriage between himself and Desdemona. Othello's power is also diminished by his failure to deconstruct the relationships between his peers and his own relationship with his aide Iago. It is further compromised by the ways his wife is silenced within the text.

If we consider shorter and more prevalent texts than *Othello*, these also deal with power. In any advert, power is always an issue: 'Your laundry will smell better than your neighbour's if you use this type of product'; 'You will attract more women if you wear this body spray'. Power is often related to ideology, or the idea of what is 'normal'. In body spray adverts, the ideology is often that of heteronormativity (discussed by Shereen Benjamin in Chapter 6): men must attract women and vice versa.

One reading of ideology in *Othello* would be that it is not normal for a black man to have more status than a white man. Another might see it as unnatural for a black man and a white woman to love each other. Some texts seek to manipulate the reader to their ideological perspective. In the case of adverts, their purpose is to sell something; in *Othello*, it is to pose a problem for the central character and audience.

Engaging in critical literacy practices forces us to consider these stances. Ira Shor (2009) explains in some detail the texts which attempted to define him and the texts which define young people in schools in New York, illustrating both the complexity and pervasive nature of text and discourse within society.

Luke (2000) also examines another important and useful idea developed through critical literacy: that text is fluid, not fixed. A text may have many different readings, depending on context – who is reading it; where is the text being read; when is the text being read; and what is the text's relationship to the world. Think about how we see female celebrities represented in media texts, which are often concerned with their physical appearance: too fat, too thin, too pale, too tanned, just right! As adults we might ignore the text's ideological message that every woman should be constantly concerned about her weight and physical appearance. An adolescent girl might have a completely different reading.

A man's reading might be different from a woman's reading. A Chinese reading might be different again.

Many classroom texts have gendered elements from which teacher and pupil have to make meaning, especially where the intended reading may be different from the negotiated reading of either teacher or learner. You might take the conversation about Lady Macbeth quoted in the introduction to this chapter as an examples of this. Here the pupil challenges a popular power-behind-the-throne reading of the play in which Macbeth is portrayed as weaker than Lady Macbeth and ultimately blamed for the murders and the chaos that ensues. In answering the teacher's question, the pupil makes a link between a problem area in the play and his perception of his mother and her power and where that power is situated.

Gaps and silences

One way of investigating text is to think about what is absent or who is absent, whose voices are heard and whose are silenced. Gaps in a text might mean that particular individuals, cultures, ideologies, genders or identities are not represented or referred to which can be linked to aspects of exclusion or marginalisation (Luke, 2000). Certain adverts that represent white middle-class families (mum, dad and two children) exclude other representations of family, whether that is in terms of race and ethnicity, class or gender. Silences are related to individuals who are located within the fabric of the text but do not have a vocal presence: they are silenced. This kind of issue can be further illustrated in the exploration of a writer's linguistic choices within a text where the word 'we' can either silence or 'give voice' to characters (Luke, 2000:2).

The reader

Critical literacy demands that we move from thinking of the reader as the traditional passive receiver of a text to someone who critically engages with it and asks questions of the text and its composer(s). This is perhaps the most exciting idea to emerge from critical literacy for teachers. If texts seek to manipulate, the reader must be aware and able to deconstruct so they can respond confidently to text. The final reading of a text by an individual reader may be compliant, negotiated or dissident.

Texts which provoke a variety of responses are often the most interesting to examine and are regularly linked to perceptions of gender, sexuality, class and race. In the film *The Blind Side* (dir. J. Hancock, 2009) the central character, a woman, is represented as a particular kind of mother, one who will fight for her child, who is a black adopted adolescent. 'Good' mothers in this film are white, affluent, beautiful and generous. 'Bad' mothers are poor, black, drug addicted, selfish and quick to abandon their children. It is clear that any audience may have a range of different readings; indeed it is hoped that an audience would not simply accept what appear to be the surface constructions of the text.

In order to negotiate or dissent from a text, however, the reader has to know what questions to ask of a text and what to do with the answers.

Taking action

The reader may choose to take action in response to a text. One example of this amongst young people in the UK was the school strike action taken by pupils in response to the Blair proposal for war in Iraq. There pupils were responding to the following texts: emails from other young people and lobbying groups; political speeches, press reports, TV documentaries and so forth.

Action might also take many other forms – from a conversation or a question, to an essay or a debate. Whatever the form, the teacher has an important role to play which relates to teaching reading (in its broadest sense) alongside informed democratic action. Such radical and effective classroom teaching will allow our teaching to become a text; a discourse about understanding power and individual worth, especially in the problematised areas of social justice.

Critical literacy questions

The key concepts outlined above suggest some broad general questions which the reader might investigate in relation to text. The following are the ones we arrived at, borrowed and currently use in much of our teaching:

■ in whose interest is this text? who benefits from this text? is anyone disadvantaged by this text?

- whose world view is privileged in this text?
- who made this text? why did they produce it in the way they have?
- how is gender constructed in this text?
- how is race constructed in this text?
- how is class constructed in this text?
- who or what has power in this text?
- whose voices are not heard in this text? are there gaps in this text. are there silences in this text?
- does this text seek to make me think in a particular way?
- are there other ways in which this text could be read?
- do I want to take action in relation to this text? what action could I take?

At this point, it might be useful to choose a text used in your classroom to see whether you can investigate it using these questions and how you may select or change them to suit your classroom context.

Critical literacy practices are used in classrooms in different parts of the world and in different contexts (Morgan, 1997). These understandings of text and reader and the importance of what is often called 'critical reading' are now emerging in curricular documents in the UK. Within the Scottish *Curriculum for Excellence*, for example, teachers are encouraged to consider a wider definition of text; teach the possibility of multiple readings of one text; consider using texts from 'popular culture' and texts which are 'relevant' (*Building the Curriculum 3* (2008) and *Literacy and English Cover Paper* (2007)). This takes us back to the main questions we address in this chapter: how can teachers 'do' social justice using this pedagogy in a classroom, and how can ITE programmes develop this kind of practice with student teachers?

Teaching teachers

We considered the problems teachers face in embedding social justice principles into their classroom teaching. Student teachers are concerned with planning – the essence of classroom life for a teacher. So this is where we, as teacher educators, began. We developed an idea which originated with Halliday (1994), and was further developed by Wallace (2009) into a planning tool.

Halliday's (1994) work in the field of linguistics emphasises the link between language and meaning. His approach recognises that social contexts shape and influence the ways in which people use language to communicate meaning. This thinking sits well within a critical literacy approach. Rather than merely focusing on the grammatical components of a language, Halliday (1994) demonstrates the systemic relation between three distinct elements that make up any given text:

- field: relates to what the text is about; what is happening within the text; what the participants are engaged in

- tenor: considers who is participating in the text; what role they play; what their relationship is with others in the text

- mode: refers to the organisation of the text and the role language plays in achieving this.

Wallace (2009) draws on Halliday and adapts his framework to enable teachers to develop critical literacy within mainstream classrooms where students are using English as an additional language (EAL). Wallace's adapted tool provides a thinking device that prompts teachers and students with EAL to consider the ways in which writers use language to convey particular types of meanings within texts. These might be in relation to issues of race, discrimination and power, for example.

We decided to utilise Wallace's adapted framework to help a small group of PGDE Secondary students to explore issues of gender while using a critical literacy approach. We refashioned some of the questions that Wallace (2009) had framed within Halliday's (1994) model and linked them to the broad components of Field, Tenor and Mode. This enabled us to integrate questions that critically explored issues of gender and analyse some of the linguistic features the writer used to achieve specific meanings at the same time.

Teaching students in the university classroom

We have used this adapted tool with various student groups but for the purposes of this chapter we will focus mainly on a small group of PGDE Secondary student teachers whom we taught prior to their first teaching practice placement. We began this process by teaching them ways in which critical literacy and gender are linked to questions of social justice. This was an overarching aim of the project and engaged them in a consideration of broader educational issues such as inclusion, equity, identity and visibility (Bernstein, 1996) in preparation for teaching in mixed-ability, multicultural secondary classrooms. Student teachers spoke about the challenges and complexities involved in connecting their concrete knowledge base to pedagogic practices in relation to social justice and gender. These mostly related to what they saw as the 'unconnectedness' of social justice to subject disciplines. Linking social justice to a specific subject was expressed as a problem and there were concerns about where it would 'fit' in teaching.

Student teachers desired not to be seen as the 'politically correct' teacher who is disrespectful to pupils' lives and does not take into account the influences on their thinking which might result in negative thoughts and behaviour around gender issues. While this position acknowledges a need to be sensitive about teaching approaches, it does not mean that teachers can choose to ignore them. Considering text with pupils – using something which is removed from the individual – can provide a safe area to discuss important matters.

We used our adapted framework to focus on critical literacy and gender. In order to contextualise the implementation of the adapted framework and to establish the relevance of the ideas we wanted to explore with the student teachers, we demonstrated how each could be linked to *Curriculum for Excellence* (CfE). During discussions student teachers made successful curricular links to citizenship and culture and felt that the existing themes that frame and permeate CfE – Successful Learners, Confident Individuals, Effective Contributors and Responsible Citizens – could easily lead to gender and cultural identity being overlooked within the current structure, despite these areas often being a source of complexity in the classroom.

We used the picture book *Into the Forest* by Anthony Browne as a semiotic tool. As secondary school teachers are not accustomed to using this type of resource as a means of exploring challenging issues, they felt somewhat out of their comfort zone and faced the same challenges school children face when encountering a new text. During the reading of the story we asked questions that linked their previous background knowledge to a critical understanding of what they would see and hear throughout the story. The table below shows the questions we asked and the student teachers' answers:

Teacher questions	Student teachers' answers
Look at the front cover. Who do you think the central character is? Is it similar to other stories you have read? Can Little Red Riding Hood be a male character? Why?	'Is that a rabbit in the shadow?' 'It's a male character, but it relates to Little Red Riding Hood.' 'Maybe ... but we think of her as a girl ... all the stories, you know.' 'It allows him to be fearful ... like in other stories.'
What aspects of Little Red Riding Hood can be seen in this text?	'He is carrying a basket and he has red shoes.' 'It is creepy, in a forest.' 'Where's the wolf?'

Student teachers seemed initially familiar with the storyline, but as they considered the text as adults rather than as children, they noticed things they had not seen before about the content of the story. This produced a fresh perspective as they interacted with the text which resulted, as the story was read aloud, in a fruitful discussion relating to the ideology that underpins traditional views of family life and gender roles.

As we read and explored each page, we asked further probing questions and drew on aspects of the Hallidayan framework as adapted by Wallace (2009) to help the student teachers develop a critical stance to the narrative as it is captured and developed within the picture book. These questions included:

- what does the colour in the story symbolise?
- who comes first in the story and why might that be?
- how is gender constructed within this part of the story?
- in whose interest is the text?
- what side of the window are you on? [a question which relates to an ambiguous double-page spread at the start of the book]

- what words (adjectives/verbs) does Browne use to construct and manipulate our reading of gender? what images does Browne use to construct and manipulate our reading of gender?
- how is the reader addressed? what pronouns are used?
- who is there, but does not speak? why might that be?
- can this text be read in different ways? is there a preferred or intended reading?

Such questions promoted an in-depth interaction with the text and student teachers commented on various features within the book in statements such as:

The colour and the shadows can represent danger.

The whole family is painted with a shadow behind it and everything is made to look small.

The author uses repetition of the phrase, 'Come home dad' and masculinity is represented as him being the breadwinner.

Are we getting his [the boy's/author's] point of view?

I can see aspects of social justice as he encounters a disadvantaged child in the forest ... the boy comforts the girl.

The mother's voice is missing – she doesn't answer the boy's questions about where the dad is.

Student teachers also raised questions about power relations between male and female characters and considered how the writer exemplified and developed them. They said that analysing the text in this way helped them to consider swapping speculative traditional and cultural views about gender. During an exploration of the themes in education related to social justice, they also identified it as part of teaching that is not separate from the curriculum, as they had previously perceived.

Once the text had been read aloud and discussed, the participants were asked to think as student teachers who were planning teaching. We asked for feedback on the type of interactions that took place during the reading of the story. These included the different responses to a range of different question types; shared exploration of ideas; and having something concrete to take thinking to and to take thinking from. All the teachers were positive in their comments about the use of the picture book for secondary pupils and noted the importance of eliciting from pupils the ways in which the themes and aspects within the text were similar to issues and experiences in their lives.

As student teachers engaged in an exploration of a text in this way, the process unlocked a lot of creativity within them as they considered various ways of thinking about their own subject and how to include a critical literacy approach to gender. Similar responses were voiced by student teachers not involved in this group, as we used the same methods in other groups. One student teacher recorded the following:

> I thought, how on earth do you make a lesson in music about gender as a matter of equality, but I can see that I could look at how women and men are characterised differently in terms of the musical instruments they play and the roles they have in performance, whether it's rock or folk or an orchestra and I could see that I would be then raising questions about gender [that could be explored] together ... and maybe challenging thinking, my own included. I like the questions we devised about 'what if?' What if we made the rock group all female with a male singer, how would that change the audience, the content of the songs, the style of music or would it affect any of these things ... why would we even notice? That fact that we notice tells us something [which] may need to be looked at. It would be interesting to teach this.

Our student teachers read through the framework again to consider which aspects they might use if they were asked to explore the movie *Shrek*. Feedback focused on ways in which to make Wallace's (2009) framework more teacher and pupil friendly, and student teachers noted the need to make the grid more practice-based.

The students' suggestions were used to devise a column of example questions which could scaffold their thinking as they considered applying such an approach in the class. Such changes to the framework will enable all pupils to access the text in meaningful ways as they explore aspects of gender (see below). During this collaboration, student teachers engaged in critical reflection as they suggested further questions and teaching strategies. These questions and strategies can be changed a little or a lot, depending on the teaching environment. The new framework therefore becomes something which can be used dynamically within a variety of situated contexts.

The student teachers were also asked to design a lesson plan, using the movie *Shrek*, which would be implemented during their first placement. They chose particular components within the new framework that seemed relevant to their pupils' needs and the aims of their lesson plan. Below is one student teacher's evaluation following a lesson which focused on the Field of Discourse.

Evaluation

Field of Discourse: Who is on top? Power relationships between men and women:

In the lesson, particularly during the feedback session where pupils presented their ideas from their pair discussions on the parodies in the clip and representation of Princess Fiona, students, especially female pupils, were keen to point out that Fiona was able to beat up Robin Hood and that Shrek and Donkey were helpless in the scene. One girl in particular was quite adamant that a girl could do this. All pupils enjoyed watching the scene for its humour and were able to pick out the parodies such as The Matrix and Crouching Tiger Hidden Dragon. When asked why they thought the director chose to represent Princess Fiona through these parodies, children responded that it was an example of satire (something I had been teaching them the meaning of, and so perhaps they said this from force of habit rather than from any deep sense of understanding) and because it is funny. They didn't comment on how the men were represented in the scene despite my prodding that Robin Hood appears quite weak when compared to Princess Fiona. This is probably because I didn't ask them to look at this aspect while they completed the mind map while watching the film.

Field of Discourse: how is gender described?:

Because they were already familiar with the film, students often commented that Fiona was a typical princess because she is pretty (in terms of her looks, clothes and hair). But because they were aware that she was an ogre as well, they also thought she was a typical ogre; her body language [was mentioned] in particular – students laughed a lot and liked to point out that she burps, for example, like the ogre Shrek. They tended to place Fiona's physical representation in relation to the Disney princesses I showed in the image at the beginning of the lesson to prove that she is like them. Many students said that she was conventional in her representation – again critical terminology and language I had been teaching them for their essay. In particular, both male and female pupils were able to comment on who the princesses were and what their stories were. They were particularly interested in the story of Mulan; one very bright female student commented that Mulan is not a typical princess because of her skin colour as well as her story because [her] primary focus is not being rescued or falling in love with a prince. The students were also interested to hear the original version of the Little Mermaid which involves a very different ending to the storyline (suicide) when compared with the Disney version. (Brian Rock, December 2011)

The student teacher's reflection identifies the ways in which schoolchildren gained insights into issues related to race, humour, behaviour and gender. A further focus on elements of language in use within the text could have been exploited by engaging them in an analysis of how the writer uses language to depict the characters within the story. This might have looked at specific linguistic features within the dialogues; explored words used to describe particular characters; or identified words that manipulate our 'reading' of gender.

Further explorations can use questioning techniques related to our adapted framework to draw out an analysis of how cultural differences influence and shape specific representations of gender. Such considerations are relevant as global migration impacts on teaching and learning contexts and classrooms become more culturally and linguistically diverse. Providing a space that encourages pupils to consider multicultural representations of gender not only enables them to gain insights into different world views, it also makes the curriculum more culturally inclusive.

In our experience of using this framework and approach in various classes, we noticed that student teachers actively planned to include elements of social justice in their classrooms. As they discussed the teaching and planning, they began to see the intersectional implications of gender, class and culture and they appeared much more reflective about the ways this impacts on their own construction of themselves as socially just teachers in the wider school.

As a result of starting from what student teachers feel they need to know – planning and lesson delivery – we return to the African proverb quoted by Rowena Arshad at the end of Chapter 1: we have been developing 'mosquito power.'

Further Reading

Janks, H (2010) *Literacy and Power*. New York: Routledge_

Shor, I (2009) What is Critical Literacy. In: Darder, A, Baltodano, M P, and Torres, R D. *The Critical Pedagogy Reader*. London: Routledge

References

Bernstein, B (1996) *Pedagogy, Symbolic Control and Identity: theory, research, critique.* London: Taylor and Francis

Browne, A (2005) *Into the Forest*. London: Walker Books

Curriculum for Excellence: all the documentation for this can be found at www.education scotland.gov.uk

Freire, P (1970) *Pedagogy of the Oppressed*. London: Penguin

Halliday, M A K (1994) *An Introduction to Functional Grammar*. London: Edward Arnold

Luke, A (2000) Critical literacy in Australia. *Journal of Adolescent and Adult Literacy* 43

Morgan, W (1997) *Critical Literacy in the Classroom: the art of the possible*. London: Routledge

Muspratt, S, Luke, A and Freebody, P (1997) *Constructing Critical Literacies*. Cresskill, N J: Rampton Press

Shor, I (2009) What is critical literacy? In Darder, A, Baltodano, M P, and Torres, R D (ed) *The Critical Pedagogy Reader*. New York and Abingdon: Routledge

Wallace, C (2009) EAL learners and critical reading. *NALDIC Quarterly* 6(3)

APPENDIX

Adapted from Wallace (2009)

Field of Discourse: Ideational Meaning – what is the text about?	Pedagogical Scaffold
In relation to gender we might consider:	− who is the main character in the text?
− who is on top? power relationships between men and women; women and women; men and men	− who do you see first in the narrative?
	− how are they described?
− whether there is a relationship between place and character – setting and representation of gender	− who has the power in the story?
	− what kind of power is it and how is it shown in the story?
− positioning of men and women in the text – are there gaps and silences in relation to voice? for example, who is there but does not speak?	− where do women and girls spend most of their time in the story?
	− is this different to the spaces where boys and men spend their time?
− language focus – how is gender described? consider the writer's word choice, tone, verbs etc.	− what characterises these spaces – what are they like?
− in whose interest is this text? what world-view is represented in terms of gender?	− whose voice do you hear in the story?
	− how much do they speak in the story?
	− who says the most in the story and why?
	− which adjectives and verbs are used to describe gender?
	− who does not speak in the story? why do they not speak?

Tenor of Discourse: Interpersonal meaning – composers to audience/ readers to text/mode of address and reader response

In relation to gender we might consider:

– what is the mode of address (omniscient, first person ...) and the implications of this for the reader?

– what is the relationship between the audience of the text and the composer(s) of the text?

– are there opportunities for multiple readings of the text?

– might the reader take a compliant, a negotiated or a dissident stance in relation to the text? (does the text allow for an authentic response from its reader?)

– in whose interest is this text?

– how does the writer tell us about the character in the text?

– what is the composer's view of the character?

– how does the writer try to make you feel about the character as you read the text – how do you know this?

– what words (adjectives/verbs/adverbs) does the writer use to make you feel this way?

– does the story change the way you feel or think if Little Red Riding Hood is a boy?

– does the text allow for multiple readings – look at the last page, is there only one answer – do you want to go back and read it to arrive at a different answer? For example, why do YOU think dad went to Grandma's house?

– who seems to have the most knowledge or understanding of things in the story – mum, dad, or the boy?

– how do you know this?

– what words or sentences give you a clue to who has the most knowledge in the story?

Mode of Discourse: How is the text organised and how can the reader approach it to make meaning?

In relation to gender we might consider:

- gender – women, men and understanding of identities – given a specific place in the structure of the text – what might this signify?

- how are participants spoken about in terms of gender – who comes first in the text (positioning) and why might that be?

- textual clutter – reading is about memory. Information from early or other bits of the text that you have to carry with you?

- weighting of voice or how information is given?

- cultural understandings of gender to make meaning from this text?

- assumptions that the writer makes about a learner's cultural understanding and world knowledge?

- what information does the writer give you first? Why does the writer do this?

- what kind of questions do you want to ask after you read/see the first page?

- what information does the writer give you at the beginning of the story that you need to remember at the end and will help you understand what has happened?

- what kind of cultural knowledge do you need to have that will help you to understand how different genders are represented within the text?

- what assumptions does the writer make about the audience in terms of cultural understandings about world knowledge?

6

'I'm not homophobic but I find this area difficult'

Shereen Benjamin

Imagine this scenario. You are sorting your class into groups for an activity. You allocate a gentle, studious boy called Callum to a group, and the boys already in that group wrinkle their noses in a display of disgust. Boys in another group laugh loudly and say 'You've got the gay boy – losers'. Later in the lesson you notice that Callum's group aren't working with him, and he has been left on the sidelines. The following day, as you walk through the playground, you see that he is on his own. Thinking about it, you can't remember the last time you saw him joining in the usual playground games. What, if anything, would you do?

Many teachers would consider Callum to be the victim of bullying, and might use their school's anti-bullying policies and practices to try to address the issue. Primary teachers might adopt whole-class problem-solving strategies, such as discussing friendship and team work in circle time or similar sessions. Secondary teachers might see it as something to be dealt with through subjects like PSHE, and might (if they considered the problem serious enough) refer the issue to guidance or pastoral specialists. The specifically homophobic component, though, is something many teachers find hard to deal with.

Research tells us that homophobic incidents frequently happen in schools without teachers noticing – or intervening. For instance, Guasp

(2009) found that although most teachers in both primary and secondary schools in her survey believed they had a duty to prevent and respond to homophobic bullying, 47 per cent of the lesbian and gay secondary school pupils interviewed for the survey said that teachers never intervened in homophobic incidents. The reasons for this non-intervention are complex: teachers may be embarrassed, may feel they lack the knowledge to approach the issue with due sensitivity, and may worry about reprisals from parents (Epstein *et al*, 2007). Schools are less likely to have policies and implementation guidelines for homophobia than they are for other dimensions of social injustice such as racism (Hunt and Jensen, 2007), and without such policies and the staffroom discussion that accompanies them, teachers may be less confident about tackling potentially difficult issues such as homophobic bullying directly with children and with the school community more broadly.

We can therefore see the importance, emphasised in other chapters of this book, of acting at school level as well as at the level of individual teachers and pupils. But important though it is to intervene when a child or young person is bullied at school and to address any homophobic element of that bullying, simply understanding the example of Callum as an incidence of homophobic bullying would be to miss an important point. Why is the word 'gay' used as an insult in Callum's classroom? How is the insult understood, and what is its significance? Why is it so powerful? And what might his teacher and the school do to challenge the assumptions and practices that made its use possible in the first place?

To answer these questions we need to think of homophobic bullying rather differently. If we begin to see homophobic bullying as an expression of fixed ideas about gender and what it means to be a 'proper boy' or 'proper girl', we can see that addressing homophobia in schools involves creating a climate where those fixed ideas can and will be challenged. In so doing, we also take a little heat out of what many teachers find a difficult and disturbing issue. This chapter explores how we might productively understand the links between homophobia and fixed ideas of gender, and considers how schools and teachers may begin to unsettle some of those ideas.

Some definitions

Whilst it is not possible in this chapter to provide definitions for all the relevant terms, it is important to define some key expressions, since anxiety about appropriate terminology can have a demonstrable impact on teachers' confidence. Being able to use terminology with confidence is also important pedagogically: as the *No Outsiders* Project Team (2010:xii) point out, there is much educational value in discussing terminology with children since it allows 'the often unspoken negative connotations these terms carry' to surface and be explored.

Here are some starting points for definitions:

- lesbian: a woman whose primary emotional and physical attraction is to women
- gay man: a man whose primary emotional and physical attraction is to men
- bisexual: someone who is emotionally and physically attracted to both women and men
- heterosexual: someone who is emotionally and physically attracted to people of the opposite sex
- transgender person (sometimes abbreviated to trans person): someone whose sense of self does not 'match' the gender they were assigned at birth. The term can also be used to describe someone who wishes to live wholly and permanently with a gendered identity other than the one they were assigned at birth and who may or may not decide to change their gender through physical interventions such as surgery
- LGBT: a commonly used abbreviation for 'lesbian, gay, bisexual and transgender'
- homophobia: fear and/or hatred of people who identify as lesbian, gay, bisexual or trans, or are perceived to do so. This umbrella term also describes any overt personal or institutional expression of prejudice or distaste
- heterocentrism: the presumption that everyone is (or in the case of children, will be) heterosexual unless otherwise stated, and the implicit or explicit belief that LGBT identities are marginal. You may see the term heteronormativity used in a similar way
- heterosexist privilege: the benefits that heterosexual people receive in a heterosexual culture, and the benefits that LGBT people may access or attempt to access as a result of claiming a heterosexual identity.

All these definitions are contested and contestable, and they change over time. Terms such as heterocentrism refer to complex sets of ideas which are explored in the rest of this chapter, and words like transgender are in fact umbrella terms which encompass many different ways in which individuals can express and live their gender. They should, therefore, be seen as starting points for thinking and for discussion with pupils and students.

Heterocentrism: homophobia as the expression of fixed ideas about gender

Why might a gentle, studious boy like Callum in the example at the beginning of this this chapter be subjected to homophobic insults? One key theorist, Raewyn Connell, developed an understanding of a hierarchy of masculinities which helps us understand the example. Connell (1995 and 2009) argues that, over time, societies that can be considered patriarchal (that is, are primarily organised by and in the interests of men) develop what she calls a 'patriarchal dividend': the privileges and benefits that men get simply by being men.

Crucially, this patriarchal dividend is not equally available to all men. Over time, societies develop 'hegemonic masculinities': those ways of being a man or a boy which are culturally exalted in their association with masculine power and prestige. If you think about the phrase 'he's a really masculine man', what comes to mind? Chances are you have thought of some of the key signifiers of hegemonic masculinity in Western societies: physical strength, sporting excellence, effortless – or apparently effortless – success, having control and/or authority and being attractive to women.

Now think of the opposite statement – 'he's not a very masculine man' or, even, 'he's an effeminate man'. What comes to mind? Perhaps you have reversed some of the qualities you first thought of and are now thinking of someone physically small, weak or vulnerable who is hopeless on the football field or rugby pitch or simply not interested in sport. You might be thinking of someone quiet who fails to assert their authority, or a person whose appearance does not conform to conventional ideas of what is heterosexually attractive. Connell and others term such representations 'subordinated masculinities'. They are not the only versions or 'modes' of masculinity in existence. Connell also describes 'protest masculinities' and 'complicit masculinities' and shows how gender intersects with other structures such as ethnicity, social class and disability to produce many different ways of being masculine.

The key point however is that these masculinities are hierarchical; hegemonic masculinities are associated with success, power and prestige, whilst their opposite, subordinated masculinities, are associated with failure, powerlessness, lack of status and femininity. This might begin to explain Callum's predicament. By engaging in a fairly routine, low-level use of homophobic language, some of the boys in the class are demonstrating their hold on high-status and heterosexualised versions of masculinity, distancing themselves from what they perceive as lower-status masculinities. To put it another way:

> boys must perform themselves as heterosexual before they can know what that might mean. In order to be recognisable as heterosexual, they may engage in signifying practices through which they abject the 'other', cast it out from the self. They may revile girls and 'sissy boys', for example, in attempts to signal, 'this is what I am not'. They accomplish this through acts that signal, 'this disgusts me'. Through such practices they may gain for themselves a sense of being heterosexual. (Davies, 2006:433)

Davies' observation reminds me of a group of primary-aged school boys I once taught in a special school. They developed a playground chasing game where the chaser would be 'gay' and whenever he caught another boy he would tap him on the arm and shout 'You're gay!' as if passing on something unclean and deeply undesirable (Benjamin, 2001). It was not meant literally that touching another boy made it likely that he would be attracted to other boys, any more than a child saying 'that pencil's gay' means that the pencil is attracted to other pencils. But by incorporating language and ideas associated with homophobia into their daily interactions and play, and by the derogation of 'gay' as weak or lame, the group highlighted how boys perform their own hold on powerful versions of masculinity and establish a heterosexualised gender identity in which homosexuality is something to be reviled and despised.

These two examples – of Callum and of my class's chasing game – show boys involved in actively producing their gendered selves in relation to wider classroom, school and society-level cultures. This is consonant with a gender relational understanding, where gender is understood as fluid and dynamic and is constantly being made and re-made by individuals, though not in conditions of their own making or choice. In the above examples, the boys negotiate a sense of self that involves participation in what Renold (2005) calls 'tough-guy masculinities'. They have not invented the narratives about masculinities and sexuality they negotiate in order to form a gendered identity; rather, those narratives – or discourses as they are sometimes known – circulate at societal level, and children's experiences of them are shaped through their social experiences in and beyond the school and their encounters with popular culture. They are also intersectional, in that gendered discourses are shaped by multiple and intersecting differences such as class, race, disability, religion and so on.

What the above examples illustrate is the inevitable interconnection between masculinity and (hetero)sexuality, through the hierarchical organisation of masculinities. This is part of a process known as heterocentrism which centralises heterosexual identities and marginalises others. Heterocentrism, like gender, does not simply exist; it needs to be re-made and re-worked through the actions of individuals.

In these examples, the boys negotiate a gendered identity by engaging in heterocentrist practices. The examples show that gaining a viable sense of self as a boy partly depends on an active and performed casting-out of homosexuality. At a school level such actions re-make a culture in which most boys are boxed in to traditional ways of being a boy and those who are unable or unwilling to conform to such 'tough-guy' versions of masculinity – because they are gentle, studious, non-sporting, too small or too big, for example – are vulnerable to ridicule and humiliation.

Are girls also subject to heterocentrist practices? The answer is yes, though in different ways. The notion of *hegemonic masculinity* does not have an exact counterpart for women and girls since hegemonic masculinities preserve male dominance and superiority. Gender relational theorists therefore talk about *emphasised femininities*: where dominant masculinities are associated with physical strength, sporting prowess, being in charge or in control and being attractive to girls/women, emphasised femininities are associated with physical weakness or aversion to participation in sports (particularly those, like football, associated with men and masculinity), being vulnerable or in need of being looked after and being attractive to boys/men.

In our supposedly post-feminist society, emphasised femininities are often translated into the femininities available to schoolgirls. A friend of mine recently tried to buy a bicycle for her granddaughter's fifth birthday. The machines designated 'for girls' were uniformly pink with pictures of Disney princesses. The machines my friend deemed gender neutral – the bright, primary-coloured ones – were in the section marked for the boys. This is a small example, but fairly typical; any visit to a toy shop or newsagent's will testify to the ubiquity of pink princess imagery for young girls. Such imagery combines the helplessness and dependency associated with emphasised femininities with the perceived have-it-all luxury lifestyle of the princess. Such a fairy tale existence is only made possible by the fulfilment of the heterocentric promise of marriage and living happily ever after.

By contrast, there are some more overtly sexualised versions of femininity which girls will routinely encounter in schools and beyond. These locate heterosexual attractiveness within a framework of glamour and the promise of fame. Such versions of femininity appear to position girls as active and in control, but do not challenge the notion that happiness and fulfillment can only or can best be achieved through being heterosexually attractive and through success in finding and keeping a desirable male partner. So we might argue that heterocentric femininities all contain elements of emphasised femininity: as with hegemonic masculinity, such femininities box girls into particular ways of expressing their gender and make life difficult for those who are unwilling or unable to be boxed in.

Negotiating heterocentric femininities can be highly complicated. For instance, although a number of commentators have associated emphasised femininity with compliance with authority, in the school setting this usually means investing in academic success. This value may be in contradiction with other values associated with emphasised femininities, such as vulnerability and vacuousness. This produces a complex web of gendered practices that girls in schools are required to negotiate.

In their study of secondary schoolgirl friendships, Currie *et al* (2007:24) found that:

> Girls must be pretty but not 'self-absorbed' about their appearance; they must be attractive to boys but not seen to be too sexually 'forward'; they must be noticed and liked by the 'right people' but not a social climber: independent but not a 'loner' and so on.

Constructing a viable gendered identity is far from straightforward for girls. A number of recent studies consider how schoolgirls use popular culture as part of their construction of their gendered and hetero-sexualised sense of self. Read (2011:9) for instance found that for the 8- and 9-year-olds in her research, 'the single most admired skill ... was the ability to sing or to dance'. She describes how these schoolgirls would act out the performances of their favourite stars, and notes how

> Such active 'performance' of sexualised femininity, often conducted in active competition with other girls, runs in tension with the passivity of the wish to 'be desired' in heteronormative ways. (Read 2011:9)

Whilst some girls can and do challenge aspects of traditional em-phasised femininities, they, like boys, are required to negotiate a set of discourses they did not create. In her study of girls in primary schools, Renold (2005:63) found that, irrespective of whether they considered themselves 'girlie' girls or not, all the girls constructed their gender identity 'in relation to a heterosexualised 'girlie' femininity' in which they were all 'investing in and policing their own and others' bodies as heterosexually desirable commodities' and in doing so were 'co-con-structing a femininity 'for the boys."

A key aspect of gender relational theory is that gender is seen as exactly that – a relation between the genders. Many commentators have noted that schoolchildren's peer relationships are inevitably understood within a heterosexual matrix (Thorne, 1993). This applies as much to single-sex friendship groups as it does to the ways in which boys and girls relate to each other. Indeed, a structuring principle of children and young people's peer group relations is boyfriend and girlfriend cultures, both within single-sex friendship groups – where heterosexual desira-bility is a popular topic of conversation and focus of attention – and mixed-gender friendships, which may automatically be branded heterosexual partnerships from a very young age. These relationships function, in part, to police the boundaries of what is acceptable gendered behaviour, and render non-heterosexualised expressions of gender undesirable. As Renold (2005) and many others have shown, girls' relational cultures are heterosexualised from a very young age and those who do not or cannot join in with 'boyfriend' talk are subject to increasing degrees of social marginalisation.

To return to my class in the special school, another key ritual the boys developed was a collective crush on a girl in an adjacent class. Joanne [not her real name] was the girl nearest in age to them who most closely embodied qualities associated with emphasised femininity. She was softly-spoken, had long hair which she spent much time brushing and styling, wore make-up when she could and had a small, slight frame. The boys would collectively follow her around the school and would often attempt to carry her belongings or appropriate them as trophies to be shown off to each other as part of a heterosexualised tough-guy peer group culture. Thus Joanne's emphasised femininity was made possible and thinkable through the actions of the boys; likewise, she enabled and made possible their particular display of dominant masculinity and the process was thoroughly heterocentric.

The point of all of this is to show that conditions for homophobia are created by particular constructions of gender. They take place in the context of wider discourses of gender that children, teachers and schools do not invent. As the examples show, children either actively take up or reject these gendered practices in local, school-specific cultures. So if we want to address the conditions which enable homophobia to flourish, we need to concentrate our efforts on heterocentric school cultures. Whilst this does not diminish the need to take robust action to challenge overtly homophobic practices where they occur, in the long run a more effective solution is to address the school cultures that enable homophobia to develop in the first place.

Changing school cultures

It is beyond the scope of this chapter to discuss curricular and pedagogic strategies for addressing heterocentrist school cultures in any detail. An increasing resource base is available in this area through books and websites: see, for instance, publications associated with the *No Outsiders* project in primary schools (DePalma and Atkinson, 2008, 2009; *No Out-*

siders Project Team, 2010), the teachers' toolkits produced by LGBT Youth Scotland (LTScotland, 2009) and teachers' guides produced by campaigning groups (eg. Stonewall, 2011). It is well worth exploring these and other resources, and referring to some general principles to think about ways you might use them in your specific context.

In what remains of this chapter, three guiding principles are explored: first, that interventions are likely to be more successful and less potentially costly or intimidating for the individual teacher when they are supported by whole-school and whole-community actions and policies; second, that explicit challenges to homophobic language and incidents, no matter how seemingly trivial, are an important part of creating a school culture that values everyone and permits a multitude of expressions of gender; and third, and perhaps most important, that challenges to a heterocentric school culture can and should be made through the curriculum.

Why is action at a whole-school and whole-community level necessary when it is possible for an individual teacher to effect a worthwhile change in their own classroom? The answer is that destabilising heterocentric cultures requires the type of deep and long-lasting change that is only likely to happen through the involvement of everyone in and around the school. This is partly a question of consistency. The individual teacher trying to challenge boyfriend and girlfriend cultures in their own class may well be undermined by the end-of-year celebration that requires children to appear with an opposite-sex partner, and awards prizes for the girl and boy most likely to stay together. But it is also about developing a structure of support around individual teachers to ensure that the discussion of difficult issues is led and managed sensitively.

Many teachers worry about a perceived cultural clash, particularly in relation to religious beliefs about sexuality. However, Epstein *et al* (2007: 81) found that engaging parents and other community members around the principle that 'children should be well-taught and happy in school' promoted genuine dialogue and positive outcomes, even where religious differences had been perceived to be problematic. Clear and unambiguous policies and policy guidelines which have involved staff, parents and children in genuinely democratic ways are therefore likely to have deep and long-lasting effects. Examples of policy documents can be found on the websites mentioned at the beginning of this section. However these should not simply be imported since the discussion and debate generated by policy-making are crucial to collective change and development.

In order to challenge heterocentric cultures, we also need to be ready to challenge homophobic incidents when they occur. While most people would agree with this in principle, research (eg. Guasp, 2009) tells us that homophobic incidents often go unchallenged in schools, with lack of confidence often a factor. When responding to a homophobic comment it can be difficult to think of a helpful response on the spur of the moment. Countless teachers have found themselves tied up in knots trying to explain to an angry or upset child or to one who maintains that they were only joking, why homophobic language is unacceptable. It is therefore helpful to think ahead and have a bank of verbal responses at the ready, and also to be willing to postpone a conversation to a quieter time, when both you and the child or young person have enough space to discuss the issue in a nuanced and sensitive way.

Some teachers may concur that when children, particularly young children, use homophobic language as a casual insult – as in, 'that pencil's so gay' – they do not mean or understand what they are saying. Here, we ought to think back to what Davies said about signifying practices. The use of the term 'gay' to mean anything weak or lame is a practice through which children – especially boys – begin to produce an inevitably heterosexual sense of self before they are aware of what it means. In a school culture where 'gay' is a routine and unchallenged insult, it can be helpful to think about the implications for the following groups of people:

- pupils who already identify as LGBT
- those who are questioning their sexuality
- those who may later come to identify as LGBT
- those who may never identify as LGBT but still do not conform to gendered expectations
- pupils who are growing up in families headed by same-sex individuals or with LGBT family members
- LGBT members of staff

■ all members of the school community who come to regard homophobic language as normal.

Seen that way, challenging every instance of homophobic language becomes an important part of creating a school culture that values everyone and challenges the fixed notions of gender discussed earlier in the chapter.

Such challenges need to be backed up by explicit teaching through the curriculum. Curricular interventions can be of many kinds. It may be useful to think of challenges to heterocentrism as being made possible through both curriculum content and curriculum structure. In the early years these are hard to separate: appropriate strategies might include the provision of books and pictures that portray a range of gendered role models and family structures, with opportunities for discussion. Other important strategies might encourage girls and boys to participate in activities traditionally associated with the opposite sex, and thinking of ways to make activities which are stereotypically gendered desirable to all children. You may want to think about which kinds of play should be encouraged and whether any should be discouraged: Browne (2004:92) points out that superhero play 'is essentially a display of hegemonic masculinity', while Paechter (2007) recommends that it should be treated cautiously and not allowed to marginalise other activities, particularly in outdoor spaces.

As children progress through primary and secondary school, the provision of resources that enable challenges to heterocentrism continues to be important. Critical literacy (discussed by Yvonne Foley and Lynne Pratt in Chapter 5) is a valuable way of enabling children and young people to recognise and explore heterocentrism. Some teachers worry about using storybooks featuring LGBT characters with primary school children, in case they are perceived to be educating children about the sexual component of same-sex relationships. Generally, such concerns are unfounded. Traditional folk tales end with the prince and princess marrying and living happily ever after; they do not go on to describe what the prince and princess did on their honeymoon. The same is true of stories and books that feature visibly LGBT characters: if the books are good, they will be relevant to the age of the children, and will not involve inappropriate sexual content or lead to inappropriate discussion.

Critical literacies are not the only possible curriculum intervention. Eisner (1985) talks about the 'null curriculum', which is what we teach pupils by what we leave out of the formal curriculum. If we do not include LGBT role models, fail to discuss the contribution of openly LGBT individuals in a range of fields and subjects, or avoid speaking about homophobia and heterocentrism directly, we may be indirectly teaching children that LGBT individuals are marginal and that LGBT issues are insignificant or taboo. Again, there is a growing resource bank for schools to help teachers incorporate anti-heterocentric content into the curriculum: LGBT History Month (2011) have sections for schools on their website, as do other campaigning organisations.

Summary

The proliferation of research and resources addressing homophobia and heterocentrism in schools during the past fifteen years is both testament to how far we have come, and an indication of how far we still have to go. A steady stream of news articles (eg. *Guardian*, 2011) reflects a growing understanding that homophobic bullying is endemic in schools and should be tackled. However, this chapter has considered homophobic incidents in school as the inevitable consequence of heterocentrism: the expression of fixed understandings of gender. A heterocentrist school environment produces the conditions in which homophobia can develop and flourish, so the trick for schools and teachers is both to challenge overt homophobia and also to effect deep and lasting change in heterocentrist school cultures. Where traditional ideas about gender are challenged, and children are not boxed into hegemonic masculinities and emphasised femininities, homophobia becomes impossible. Whilst this aspiration may not be fully achievable quite yet, it is nonetheless a worthwhile aspiration. Even its partial realisation is likely to result in positive change for all children.

Further Reading

No Outsiders Project Team (2010) *Undoing Homophobia in Primary Schools*. Stoke-on-Trent, Trentham

Rasmussen, M L (2006) *Becoming Subjects: sexualities and secondary schooling*. London, Routledge

References

Benjamin, S (2001) Challenging masculinities: disability and achievement in testing times. *Gender and Education* 13(1) p39-55

Browne, N (2004) *Gender Equity in the Early Years*. Maidenhead: Open University Press

Connell, RW (1995) *Masculinities.* Cambridge: Polity

Connell, R (2009) *Gender.* Cambridge, Polity

Currie, D, Kelly, D and Pomerantz, S (2007) 'The power to squash people': understanding girls' relational aggression. *British Journal of Sociology of Education* 28(1) p23-37

Davies, B (2006) Subjectification: the relevance of Butler's analysis for education. *British Journal of Sociology of Education* 27(4) p425-438

DePalma, R and Atkinson, E (ed) (2008) *Invisible Boundaries: addressing sexualities equality in children's worlds.* Stoke on Trent: Trentham Books

DePalma, R and Atkinson, E (ed) (2009) *Interrogating Heteronormativity in Primary Schools: the No Outsiders project.* Stoke on Trent: Trentham Books

Eisner, E (1985) *The Art of Education.* Lewes: Falmer

Epstein, D, Hewitt, R, Leonard, D, Mauthner, M and Watkins, C (2007) Confronting homophobia in UK schools: taking a back seat to multicultural and antiracist education. In van Dijk, L and van Driel, B (eds) *Challenging Homophobia: teaching about sexual diversity.* Stoke on Trent: Trentham Books

The Guardian (2011) Why is school such a hard place to be gay? 10 November 2011

Guasp, A (2009) *The Teachers' Report: homophobic bullying in Britain's schools.* London: Stonewall, http://www.stonewall.org.uk/education_for_all/research/2731.asp (accessed 11 Nov 2011)

Hunt, R and Jensen, J (2007) *The School Report: the experiences of young gay people in Britain's schools.* London: Stonewall, http://www.stonewall.org.uk/education_for_all/research/1790.asp (accessed 11 Nov 2011)

LGBT History Month (2011) For schools, http://lgbthistorymonth.org.uk/for-schools/ (accessed 11 Nov 2011)

LTScotland (2009) *Toolkit for Teachers: dealing with homophobia and homophobic bullying in Scottish schools,* Glasgow, Learning and Teaching Scotland. http://www.ltscotland.org.uk/Images/LGBT%20low%20res%207%2701%2709_tcm4-512286.pdf (accessed 11 Nov 2011)

No Outsiders Project Team (2010) *Undoing Homophobia in Primary Schools.* Stoke on Trent: Trentham Books

Paechter, C (2007) *Being Boys, Being Girls: learning masculinities and femininities.* Maidenhead: Open University Press

Read, B (2011) Britney, Beyoncee and me – primary school girls' role models and constructions of the 'popular' girl. *Gender and Education* 23(1) p1-13

Renold, E (2005) *Girls, Boys and Junior Sexualities: exploring children's gender and sexual relations in the primary school.* Abingdon, RoutledgeFalmer

Stonewall (2011) *Challenging Homophobic Language.* Stonewall Education Guides. Available from http://www.stonewall.org.uk/media/current_releases/3606.asp (accessed 28 Feb 2012)

Thorne, B (1993) *Gender Play: girls and boys in school.* Buckingham, Open University Press

7

Inclusive practices for pupils with English as an additional language

Andy Hancock

Introduction: multilingual classrooms

The need for teachers to take account of the diverse nature of their schools continues to grow as the scale and scope of migration transforms the linguistic makeup of classrooms. The linguistic landscape of the UK has been characterised for nearly half a century by large settled communities of citizens originally from commonwealth countries such as Pakistan, India, the Caribbean, Bangladesh and Hong Kong. More recently, the expansion of the European Union in 2004 and 2007 brought a substantial, and largely unexpected, arrival of migrant workers especially from Poland seeking employment, who contribute to the country's economy and whose children have added to the richness of multilingual classrooms.

Furthermore, political and economic instability across the globe have seen the arrival of significant numbers of refugee and asylum-seeking families to our shores. Most of the families originate from countries experiencing conflict (such as Afghanistan, Somalia and Zimbabwe) or persecution (such as the Roma in Eastern Europe and the Kurds in Iraq). Many of these pupils, including unaccompanied young people, may have additional challenges such as low literacy levels due to gaps in their formal schooling in their own country or in countries where they lived in transit. These pupils may also require pastoral care for emotional and psychological issues as a result of experiencing trauma and suffering from distress (Rutter, 2003).

Another distinct group are 'elite' bilingual pupils whose parents travel for business, academic and diplomatic reasons. These families may have short-term residence and the children's acquisition of English is frequently viewed as an advantageous educational resource in an increasingly globalised world.

All these forms of global migration are characterised by the notion of 'super-diversity' (Vertovec, 2007). This is distinguished by a dynamic interplay of variables among an increased number of new and scattered, multiple-origin, socio-economically differentiated and legally stratified migrants. As a result the changing pattern of linguistic diversity, most teachers will encounter multilingual classrooms at some point in their careers and when they do, they need to feel confident and equipped with the knowledge and skills to address the needs – and talents – of learners for whom English is an additional language (EAL).

This chapter does not give details of the strategies to support additional language acquisition as this has been covered comprehensively elsewhere, but it does refer readers to some key sources of guidance. The primary aim of the chapter is to provide a brief sketch of some of the main theoretical understandings that underpin the area of EAL and to highlight some of the challenges facing teachers. It also offers guidance to monolingual and student teachers on inclusive practices, as part of a wider social justice agenda for schools, in order to promote children's self-esteem, participation and achievement. The text is interspersed with short illustrative examples that draw on authentic school and classroom events to highlight potential tensions. These are followed by reflective questions to stimulate critical discussion and debate.

Asking questions and gathering information

The Education (Additional Support for Learning) Act 2004 introduced a new framework in Scotland to provide for children and young people who require additional support with their learning, and for the first time includes those with EAL. The accompanying Code of Practice (2005) contains the following advice:

A need for additional support does not imply that a child or young person lacks abilities and skills. For example, bilingual children or young people, whose first language is not English, may already have a fully developed home language and a wide range of achievements, skills and abilities. Any lack of English should be addressed within a learning and teaching programme which takes full account of the individual's abilities and learning needs. (Scottish Executive, 2005:20)

This discourse clearly acknowledges the *linguistic capital* bilingual pupils bring to a school which can act as a foundation for teaching and learning. Although the legislation has rightly raised the profile of EAL learners, it is important to stress the obvious but crucial point that they are not homogeneous. They do not have the same needs and experiences. They range from new arrivals to a pool of second or third generation British-born learners, many of whom speak English to their siblings at home but may still require language support to develop their full academic potential.

It is important to understand the heterogeneous nature of minority ethnic communities in the UK in terms of migration histories, sociolinguistic profiles, beliefs and attitudes; and how these lived experiences and changing proficiencies, allegiances and affiliations to different languages and literacies are inextricably linked with dynamic and complex identities (see Hancock, 2006).

It is not enough to argue that policies must meet the needs of learners with EAL; information must be detailed enough to pick up the uniqueness between and within minority groups and differentiate support for individuals and families accordingly. When a school encounters a new pupil with EAL, background information should be acquired upon enrolment with the help of a trained interpreter (for guided questions and procedures on initial assessment, see Hall, 2001; Howard, 2008.)

However, teachers also need to engage learners with EAL and this implies taking a listening stance and viewing classrooms as places where not only children learn but where teachers can also gain valuable knowledge about individual children's linguistic and cultural capital. How teachers can apply these intercultural insights to their own teaching practice is the focus of another section in this chapter.

The concept of intersectionality is helpful here to gain an understanding of how race and ethnicity affect children and young people's experiences and educational outcomes. There is a need to consider other aspects of the learner's identity such as gender, place of birth, age of migration, educational background and religion and cultural heritage. Moreover, attention also needs to be paid to factors which impact on childhood circumstances such as family structure, family income, geographical location, health, parents' educational background and parental aspirations for their children (see Emejulu, 2008).

The policy context of language in education

The vast majority of families who belong to linguistic minorities are keen to maintain the language of the home as it is integral to their identity, home literacy practices and cultural heritage. However, within the current policy context, these young people with EAL are faced with two competing languages, one of which is the language of education and power. There is therefore a strong incentive for those in the language minority to learn the language of power in order to participate fully in society. In this situation, they risk losing their home language, which is often perceived by wider society as a low status language. According to García (2009), the language shift will be complete within three generations, and the third generation will lose the ability to communicate in what was the family's home language. That is to say the educational outcome is monolingualism, or at best limited bilingualism, where learners are forced to assimilate into the majority language and culture as soon as possible.

The reality of this policy context means linguistic minority pupils face a number of challenges. First, they are 'submerged' into a new language in mainstream classrooms and face the dual task of learning English while attempting to access the curriculum through this new or developing language. Second, these pupils frequently do not have sufficient competency in English to interact with native-speaking peers who provide important friendships and good models of the target language. Third, they must quickly adapt to a learning and teaching environment which may be culturally unfamiliar. Gaine (2005) also asserts that these pupils experience racism on a regular basis, which impacts on their self-esteem and learning.

Bilingual pupils are also competing with a moving target as their mono-lingual peers continue to make progress academically (Thomas and Collier, 2002). Anecdotal evidence suggests that pupils with EAL are fre-quently assigned to low-ability groups and given academically inappro-priate work; moreover, their poor performance on assessments designed for monolingual native speakers of English confirms their teachers' low expectations. The Educational Inspectorate in Scotland has recognised the growing need for schools to take more responsibility for evaluating their educational provision for bilingual learners and guidelines have been produced outlining effective ways to self-monitor this (HMIE, 2006). A further document (HMIE, 2009) seeks to inform schools on good practice and areas for development when working with recently arrived children and families.

Language-sensitive pedagogy

For language support to be effective, it cannot be taught using the tradi-tional methodology for modern foreign languages, namely through a discrete set of skills in a prescriptive step-by-step fashion, using text-books and employing a progression of discrete grammar-translation rules. The practice of placing some new arrivals into separate schools or language classes has also been condemned, with such segregated pro-vision viewed as a form of institutionalised racism. The argument put forward here is that withdrawing children and young people from mainstream classrooms results in stigmatisation and reinforces a sense of deficit. The provision also restricts pupils' contact with English-speaking peers and access to the full curriculum available in main-stream classrooms.

The preferred support model involves full inclusion of pupils in main-stream classrooms from the start, with an accompanying strategic whole-school approach which views inclusion as the responsibility of all prospective and practising teachers. Organisations like NALDIC (http://www.naldic.org.uk) take the position that effective language support incorporates the interwoven elements of social, cultural, cogni-tive and linguistic development.

The challenge for teachers is how to promote language-sensitive teach-ing so that the pupil develops important relationships with English-speaking peers and is stretched both linguistically and cognitively at their appropriate level. This can be achieved by class and subject teachers having high expectations and creating opportunities for pupils to activate prior knowledge. It involves learning both English and curriculum content simultaneously, through collaborative learning tasks using knowledge frameworks, graphic organisers and key visuals. (For detailed explanations of these methodologies see Brent Language Service, 1999 and Mohan, 2001.)

The argument here is that by using scaffolding strategies and adjusting classroom pedagogies in this way, teachers can make learning more accessible, with benefits to bilingual and monolingual pupils alike. There is no space here for details of planning for language and content teaching, but for advice on supporting new arrivals see Gibbons 1993 and DfES 2007. For guidance on appropriate pedagogy see Smyth 2003; Learning and Teaching Scotland 2005 and 2006; Leung and Creese 2010. Examples of subject-specific pedagogies for teaching EAL pupils can be found in *Access and Engagement in Design and Technology* (DfES, 2002a) and *Access and Engagement in Physical Education* (DfES, 2002b).

Language proficiency – how long does it take?

The stages of additional language acquisition are well documented, using a continuum of New to English (including an initial 'Silent Period'),

---

Roxanna is 9 years of age and recently arrived from Iran. She speaks Farsi to her sister and parents at home. The class teacher believes Roxanna needs support with her English reading and she has organised for Roxanna to work through an individualised phonics programme on the computer in the corner of the classroom while the rest of the class are engaged in collaborative group activities based on the class topic looking at the language and layout of adverts from magazines. It soon becomes apparent that Roxana spends a lot of the time turning away from the computer to watch what her peers are doing.

How can class teachers ensure that new arrivals are included in mainstream activities while having appropriate support tailored to their individual needs?

How can opportunities be created for Roxanna to be involved in the topic work of the class to ensure both language and cognitive development?

Early Acquisition, Developing Competence, Competent and Fluent. For support strategies at each of these stages see http://www.ealedinburgh. org.uk/. Although these five phases provide a useful sequential framework it is worth remembering that the 'average' pupil with EAL does not exist: they enter school at different ages, from a variety of backgrounds and with different personalities. That said, it is important to distinguish between language used for social purposes – or the language of the playground – and to the academic language required to access the curriculum. Cummins (2000) believes that it takes pupils with EAL about eighteen months to two years to acquire Basic Interpersonal Communication Skills (BICS) but it may take five to seven years or longer for some pupils with EAL to achieve Cognitive Academic Language Proficiency (CALP).

Assessing pupils with EAL based purely on their apparent conversational fluency may mask their need for continued support with language and literacy in classrooms where the language used is more abstract and demanding. In the period after pupils develop everyday conversational and transaction English but before they acquire

---

Akiko is a 15-year-old new arrival from Japan. Her subject teachers are called to a meeting by the Senior Management Team to discuss her timetable and induction. During the meeting, Anne, the Physical Education teacher, asks if there is any EAL support available for the PE lessons. The answer is that the EAL teacher has to prioritise and will only be supporting Akiko in History and Biology. Anne is concerned that Akiko's participation in PE may have health and safety implications as Akiko will not be able to understand instructions during the practical lessons. Furthermore, the class are doing a unit on exercise and the cardiovascular system and Anne feels that the language contained in the unit will be too difficult for Akiko.

What provision and support should be made for new arrivals in and outside PE lessons?

How can teachers find time to consult and plan alongside EAL support teachers?

How do subject teachers ensure language-sensitive teaching and learning takes place in their curriculum area?

academic English, there is a danger that their teachers may assume that they are falling progressively behind their monolingual peers, and the pupils may lose confidence and motivation because of lack of success. Furthermore, the poor academic performance of pupils who appear comfortable in English may give teachers the sense that the child is not trying or has a learning difficulty. The challenge for teachers is to provide appropriate modified activities that are cognitively demanding and linguistically accessible without being over-simplified. (For examples of differentiated tasks see Cooke, 2005.)

Translanguaging

More often than not, the education system treats the two languages of the bilingual pupil separately and the monolingual teacher focuses on the problems that the lack of English causes. There is often a misconception that bilingualism confuses pupils and that parents using languages other than English at home delay the acquisition of the language of schooling. By contrast, Cummins (2000) prefers to see the languages as interwoven and uses the iceberg analogy to illustrate this point. The two peaks of the iceberg above the waterline represent the distinct surface features of the different languages but underneath the water the two languages share a common underlying proficiency which allows concepts and skills to be transferred from one language to another. For example, a Polish child who has already received an education in Poland will have already developed literacy skills such as decoding an alphabetic script. They will not have to learn to read again but will merely have to adapt their decoding skills to the phonology or sound system of English when reading. They will require additional support with the comprehension of English texts. For example, pupils will not have the depth of vocabulary to make sense of the new words they are reading or the cultural knowledge to gain meaning from some of the stories to which they are exposed in school.

Teachers need to look beyond the monolingual classroom context for creative opportunities that allow pupils with EAL to draw on all their linguistic resources for learning purposes across the curriculum. García (2009) calls this *translanguaging*, where pupils are active agents and can use the languages at their disposal on their own terms. Translanguaging views code-switching as a natural phenomenon in multilingual settings and an integral part of pupils' identity formation. It is also evident that their flexible bilingualism performs an important function as a tool for thinking and literacy learning (Hancock, 2011). The teacher taps into the children's pre-existing cultural and linguistic knowledge and draws on the pupils' bilingual skills to support the discussion of concepts and skills.

Teachers can make choices and transform classroom practices by drawing on the home language in many ways, for example:

- use bilingual staff
- invite parents to read stories in their home language
- invite parents to support children's learning through first language
- allow pupils to use dual-language dictionaries
- build up a dual-language library of books and audio tapes
- paired reading of bilingual books with a buddy who shares the same language
- encourage children to write and publish bilingual/multilingual texts
- share resources and develop teaching and learning through video conferencing
- make displays that incorporate a variety of languages and scripts
- celebrate children's accomplishments gained at complementary schools and acknowledge their biliteracy talents within individual learning portfolios
- learn key words in child's home language.

Each of these actions challenges the dominant educational discourse that claims that developing a child's first language hinders the learning of English. Teachers can also gain knowledge of the cultural and linguistic capital which bilingual pupils bring to school. Changing classroom pedagogies by using the aforementioned strategies will not only raise awareness of language diversity among the monolingual school population, it will also have a positive impact on intercultural sensitivity and language awareness.

In the staffroom Rachael, a class teacher, is talking to her colleague Juliet. She mentions that she observed Martyn and Frideryk whispering in Polish to each other during their number work. Rachael says, 'I told them you can't speak Polish here. They can't speak English properly and they really need to practice it.'

If you were the other member of staff listening to Rachael how would you respond to her view?

How can an ethos be created so pupils feel comfortable using their first language in the classroom without this creating a barrier to other members of the class?

Authors such as Baker (2011) have refuted earlier claims about language confusion in bilingual pupils and point to the various intellectual and literate advantages to the individual when conditions are favourable to bilingual development. Enhanced vocabularies and wider phonological systems give bilingual children metalinguistic awareness – that is, the ability to talk about language and how it works and a facility for learning further languages. Additionally, the experience of learning two languages gives bilingual pupils well-developed problem-solving skills and creative abilities and a strong potential for cross-cultural empathy.

The attitudes towards languages in society are frequently determined by shifting ideologies mediated through socio-economic considerations and politics, rather than a concern for social justice and the educational enrichment of bilingualism. Suddenly a language which has been discounted and neglected by the school system as a vernacular of a cultural minority takes on high economic status. For example, China's re-emerging position of strength within global economics and trading systems has produced demands, within both business and political circles, for Chinese to be taught in schools to foster economic co-operation with China. This is not unlike the promotion of Japanese in a few British schools in the 1990s which was intended to support commercial activity with Japan. However, it is disappointing if bilingualism is promoted only in such circumstances, rather than viewing it as an asset in itself within wider social contexts.

Hakim is 14 years old and has just arrived from Malaysia. He will be in your school for a year while his mother undertakes an MSc programme at the local university. The Deputy Headteacher, who has responsibility for time-tabling, has arranged for Hakim to be withdrawn from modern languages, in order to have individual tuition to develop his English language skills. This support will be provided by the Additional Support Needs (ASN) teacher in the Support for Learning base. The DHT says Hakim needs to concentrate on learning English and introducing another language through English will only confuse him. When asked by the ASN teacher about his new school, Hakim says he would like to learn French as he enjoys learning languages. The teacher discovers Hakim can converse in English because it is a compulsory subject at primary and secondary schools in Malaysia. As a Muslim he regularly reads the Qu'ran in Arabic. In addition, Malaysia has a large Chinese population and Hakim knows some Cantonese because of his Chinese friends at school.

What might be done so that Hakim has the opportunity to learn French and develop his English?

How do you know what knowledge and experiences the pupils with EAL bring to your school?

Few opportunities are presently available within mainstream schools for speakers of minority languages to develop their first language skills. The context of this policy and of coercive power relations means that countries such as Scotland are currently not in a favourable position to capitalise on their linguistic resources. Teachers may also encounter a number of contradictory discourses currently being played out within political and educational forums. On the one hand, there have been moves towards embedding citizenship education within the main-stream curriculum with an emphasis on informed decision-making and taking thoughtful and responsible action. This will act as a catalyst to encourage children and young people to actively engage in issues of social justice and intercultural encounters at local, national and global levels.

On the other hand, there has been a political rebranding of the notion of citizenship, in response to the challenges presented through increasing levels of diversity. The UK government's prioritisation of a community cohesion agenda aims to counter the perceived challenges that migrants pose to a cohesive 'national cultural identity' where differences are seen as dangerous. The result is the enforcement of English language and citizenship testing for new migrants seeking to gain right of residence. This construct of national identity as a political ideology sends powerful messages to educators when citizenship requirements are made conditional on proficiency in the 'official' language. The policy of using language to legitimise or de-legitimise people only reinforces assimilationist and monolingual agendas rather than valuing linguistic pluralism.

Partnerships with parents

Parents have tremendous knowledge of their own children, and research shows that minority ethnic parents have a deep-seated interest in their children's education. This should be viewed as an important resource. It is important for schools to engage with parents and respect them as equal partners. Teachers need to listen to parents and learn to appreciate the home background and daily lives of the diverse community the school serves. The primary focus should be on involving schools with parents, rather than merely demanding that parents engage with school.

There are inherent dangers in making assumptions about parents' educational beliefs based on their cultural background. Teachers need to recognise that cultures are dynamic and they should strive to avoid seeing minority ethnic parents as one homogeneous group. Parental partnership is a process where both parents and teachers work towards an achievable sharing of power and responsibility, and consultation with parents should be conducted in the spirit of respectful dialogue and learning from each other.

Whilst, effective dialogue encourages the interchange of ideas and opinions, this type of communication also requires the use of trained and professional interpreters if parents have limited English. No two families are the same but Moskal's (2010) research with the Polish community in Scotland highlighted some of the common issues and barriers minority families experience that hinder them from being fully involved in their children's schooling.

Ca Mei is a Cantonese-speaking 5-year-old girl. A meeting has been arranged through an interpreter with her parents in the morning because the parents work unsocial hours in the family-run take-away. Maureen, the class teacher, is concerned that Ca Mei doesn't speak much in class and is therefore missing out on opportunities to interact with her peers and form friendships.

What questions would you like to ask Ca Mei's parents whilst sharing your knowledge of Ca Mei in an open and collaborative manner?

How can you develop your skills in active listening and working in partnership with interpreters?

When communicating with minority parents, how can you ensure that your own beliefs and values are not conveyed to the parents, either consciously or subconsciously?

Summary

This chapter has drawn attention to the challenges teachers face in increasingly diverse classrooms and to the contribution teachers can make in supporting pupils with EAL to be effective learners. It has been shown that by building on the full range of languages that learners of EAL have at their disposal, conditions can be created to enable both their language and their academic development. Furthermore, it was argued that adjusting classroom pedagogies in this way will benefit not only learners of EAL but all learners. I hope after reading this, that student teachers and teachers will feel more confident and better equipped with the knowledge and skills to respond positively to the reality of multilingual classrooms.

Further Reading

Haslam, L, Wilkin, Y and Kellet, E (2006) *English as an Additional Language: Meeting the Challenge in the Classroom.* London: David Fulton

Leung, C and Creese, A (eds) (2010) *English as an Additional Language: Approaches to Teaching Linguistic Minority Students.* London: Sage

References

Baker, C (2011) *Foundations of Bilingual Education and Bilingualism* (5th edn). Clevedon: Multilingual Matters

Brent Language Service (1999) *Enriching Literacy: text, talk and tales in today's classroom: a practical handbook for multilingual schools.* Stoke on Trent: Trentham Books

Coles, S (2008) Pupils' experiences of racism. In Statham, L. (ed) *Counting Them In: isolated bilingual learners in schools.* Stoke on Trent: Trentham Books

Cooke, S (2005) *Collaborative Learning in the Classroom*, Guidance Document 9. City of Nottingham Education Department

Cummins, J (2000) *Language, Power and Pedagogy: bilingual children in the cross-fire.* Clevedon: Multilingual Matters

DfES (2002a) *Access and Engagement in Design and Technology: teaching pupils for whom English is an additional language.* London: DfES

DfES (2002b) *Access and Engagement in Physical Education: teaching pupils for whom English is an additional language.* London: DfES

DfES (2007) *New Arrivals Excellence Programme: Guidance.* London: DfES

Emejulu, A (2008) The intersection of ethnicity, poverty and wealth. In Ridge, T and Wright, S (ed) *Understanding Inequality, Poverty and Wealth.* Bristol: Policy Press

Gaine, C (2005) *We're All White, Thanks: the persisting myth about 'white' schools.* Stoke on Trent: Trentham Books

García, O (2009) *Bilingual Education in the 21st Century: a global perspective.* Oxford: Blackwell

Gibbons, P (1993) *Learning to Learn in a Second Language.* Portsmouth: Heinemann

Hall, D (2001) *Assessing the Needs of Bilingual Pupils: living in two languages* (2nd edn). London: David Fulton

Hancock, A (2006) Attitudes and Approaches to Literacy in Scottish Chinese Families. *Language and Education* 20(5) p355-373

Hancock, A (2011) Unpacking mundane practices: children's experiences of learning literacy at a Chinese Complementary School in Scotland. *Language and Education*, DOI: 10.1080/09500782.2011.609280

HM Inspectorate of Education (2006) *Inclusion and Equality: evaluating educational provision for bilingual learners.* Edinburgh: HMIE

HMIE (2009) *Count Us In: meeting the needs of children and young people newly arrived in Scotland.* Livingston: HM Inspectorate of Education

Howard, J (2008) Assessing isolated bilingual learners. In Statham, L (ed) (2008) *Counting Them In: isolated bilingual learners in schools.* Stoke on Trent: Trentham Books

Learning and Teaching Scotland (2005) *Learning in 2+ Languages.* Dundee: LTS (Now available from www.educationscotland.gov.uk)

Learning and Teaching Scotland (2006) *Languages for Life: Across the 3-18 curriculum.* Dundee: LTS (Now available from www.educationscotland.gov.uk)

Leung, C and Creese, A (ed) (2010) *English as an Additional Language: approaches to teaching linguistic minority students.* London: Sage

Mohan, B (2001) The second language as a medium of learning. In Mohan, B, Leung, C and Davison, C (ed) *English as a Second Language in the Mainstream: teaching, learning and identity.* London: Longman

Moskal, M (2010) Polish Migrant Children's Experiences of Schooling and Home-School Relations in Scotland. *Briefing Report 54.* University of Edinburgh

Rutter, J (2003) *Supporting Refugee Children in 21st Century Britain.* Stoke on Trent: Trentham Books

Scottish Executive (2005) *Additional Support for Learning:Code of Practice.* Edinburgh: Scottish Executive

Smyth, G (2003) *Helping Bilingual Pupils to Access the Curriculum.* London: David Fulton

Thomas, WP and Collier, VP (2002) *A National Study of School Effectiveness for Language Minority Students' Long-term Academic Achievement.* Santa Cruz, CA: Center for Research on Education, Diversity and Excellence, University of California-Santa Cruz

Vertovec, S (2007) Super-diversity and its implications. *Ethnic and Racial Studies* 30(6) p1024-1054

8

Challenging Islamophobia:
a whole-school approach

Paul Vernell

Setting the context

Islamophobia is not a new phenomenon. Anti-Muslim sentiment can be traced back as far as the early Middle Ages. The first crusade to 'recapture the Holy Land' began in November 1095. The *Reconquista* (re-conquest) of Spain in 1492 ended the ascendancy of the Islamic world.

However, as a current dominant form of the new racism based on perceived cultural differences and hostility to an undifferentiated Muslim identity, Islamophobia has a more recent history. Certainly the West's response to the Iranian revolution and the appearance of three million Iranians on the streets of Teheran welcoming the return of the Ayatollah Khomeini in 1979 marked a turning point in the discourses associated with anti-Muslim ideology (Abbas, 2005:13).

The publication of Salman Rushdie's *Satanic Verses* a decade later in 1989 is another key moment in the proliferation of anti-Muslim rhetorical strategies in Britain. This work of fiction became a site of struggle between the Muslims who saw it as a blasphemous insult and the liberal – and not so liberal – defenders of the right to freedom of expression. Public protests against the novel allowed the media to circulate a new image of 'intolerant Muslims'. Nearly a decade later again, the

Runnymede Trust identified the motifs of this new rhetoric (Runnymede Trust, 1997).

Firstly, as with the creation of all *others*, Islam is seen as homogeneous and static: there is only one Islam and it never changes. Secondly, there is seen to be a politico-military agenda behind Islam: the 'colonisation' of the West motivated by an implacable opposition to Western values and mores (Abbas, 2005:12). Next, the report noted, this perceived colonisation of Western space allowed it to be implicated in the anti-immigration discourse exploited by both New Labour and the current coalition government in order to manage discontent over the invasion of Iraq and, more recently, labour market insecurities.

All this was fuelled in the wake of 9/11. A narrative that had increasingly moved centre stage now came to dominate the media. A violent 'mad' fanaticism, intolerant and virulently anti-democratic, was now the lens through which to view Islam. This representation became known as 'political Islam' or simply 'fundamentalism' (Seymour, 2010:80). The sub-narrative of the so-called 'war on terror' has been with us now for over a decade. It has become the discursive context for national policy initiatives. The discourse of *community cohesion*, a Labour government response to the Northern riots of 2001 sparked by National Front attacks on local Asian communities in towns such as Bolton and Bradford, re-presented the victims of racial violence and marginalisation as the agents of their own victimhood (Cantle, 2001). These representations have been counterposed by the Runnymede Trust with more open and fluid approaches.

This approach has begun to influence education policy and many local authorities have encouraged schools to take the ideas implicit within it

Eight distinctions between an open and closed view of Islam

Distinctions	Closed views on Islam	Open views on Islam
Monolithic/diverse	Islam seen as a single monolithic block, static and unresponsive to new realities	Islam seen as diverse and progressive with internal differences, debates and perspectives

Distinctions	Closed views on Islam	Open views on Islam
Separate/interacting	Islam seen as separate and a) not having any aims or values in common with other cultures b) not affected by them c) not influencing them	Islam seen as interdependent with other faiths and cultures a) having certain shared values and aims b) affected by them c) enriching them
Inferior/different	Islam seen as inferior to the West, barbaric, irrational, primitive, sexist	Islam seen as distinctly different, but not deficient, and as equally worthy of respect
Enemy/partner	Islam seen as violent, aggressive, threatening, supportive of terrorism, engaged in a 'clash of the civilisations'	Islam seen as an actual or potential partner in joint co-operative enterprises and in the solution of shared problems
Manipulative/sincere	Islam seen as political ideology, used for political or military advantage	Islam seen as a genuine religious faith, practised sincerely by its adherents
Criticism of West rejected/considered	Criticism made by Islam of 'the West' rejected out of hand	Criticisms of 'the West' and other cultures are considered and debated
Discriminating defended/criticised	Hostility towards Islam used to justify discriminatory practices towards Muslims from mainstream society	Debates and disagreements with Islam do not diminish efforts to combat discrimination and and exclusion

Distinctions	Closed views on Islam	Open views on Islam
Islamaphobia seen as natural/problematic	Anti-Muslim hostility accepted as natural and 'normal'	Critical views of Islam are themselves subjected to critique, lest they be inaccurate and unfair

Source: Runnymede Trust (1997) Islamophobia: A challenge for us all. London: Runnymede Trust

seriously. As with all national policy initiatives, its translation into policy and practice at school level has been highly uneven. Nevertheless, at a conference on *Challenging Racism* called by South Gloucestershire NUT in February 2010 the lack of guidance and clarity led participants, many of whom were young teachers, to register their feeling that they were unprepared for the challenges of confronting Islamophobia in the classroom.

Enlisted into the rhetoric of community cohesion, teachers wanted to 'do something' but were lacking models of what a curriculum that engaged with the racism of school communities might look like, particularly in majority white schools. They were unsure about how to respond to the practicalities of challenging rising Islamophobia. Was a multicultural approach sufficient or was a more explicit antiracist curriculum needed? And was a different pedagogy needed?

Models of learning

Models of learning that dominate in schools are never static, though there are many surveillance systems in place to keep an eye on 'standards' and ensure that not too much innovation or creativity takes place. Nonetheless, alongside the 'common sense' of input-output models of curriculum 'delivery' that are currently hegemonic, there is a 'good sense' that sits alongside and which is often felt by teachers to be at odds with the officially authorised technologies of teaching and learning (Gramsci, 1971:325-334). This is because most teachers have a broader understanding of what constitutes education than the increasingly narrow conception that is held by the Department for Education.

For as teachers learn to negotiate a world of economic turmoil which is resulting in mass unemployment (and recent figures estimate that youth unemployment stands at 22% for 16 to 24 year olds) the debate about education's purposes is dominated by ideas of employability.

In the light of this, the official 'basics' curriculum sits inside teachers' minds alongside ideas that education should:

- be about the whole person
- enable participation, transformation and enjoyment of the world
- focus on the critical testing of received *doxa*
- develop collaboration in testing solutions to real moral and practical issues.

This good sense, developed out of the *collective experience* of working in the day-to-day reality of schools, challenges the individualised con-sumerist model of education with one in which the learner is the agent of learning in a reciprocal process with peers, community and teachers. As Freire notes in *Pedagogy of the Oppressed* (1996:60-61), this approach begins to deconstruct the dichotomy between educator and educated and challenges schools to become sites in which both staff and students are learners and everyone educates each other through their inter-actions with the wider community.

One school that has attempted this model of learning is Abbeywood Community School (formerly Filton High School) in South Gloucester-shire. Here, a group of teaching and non-teaching staff initiated a net-work called Alternative Futures. The group came together after the tsunami hit South East Asia in 2004. Many students were concerned about the effects of the tsunami and were interested in scientific, prac-tical, moral and political issues, thrown up by the disaster. In January 2005 the school decided to suspend the curriculum for a week and all faculties planned lessons to allow each year group to enquire exten-sively into the event. The decision also offered students an opportunity to devise responses to the tragedy.

On a number of occasions since then, the group have consciously set out to offer a different model of learning, one that does not just recon-figure the space and time of established school routines but tries to recast a hands-on social justice model of curriculum design linked to topical issues. In 2009 the school organised a cultural diversity and antiracism fortnight for Year 9 students.

Themed learning

In themed learning a school works with learners on identifying a thread – in this case racism – and subject areas work towards a whole school outcome. Faculties plan a series of lessons that will empower students to engage with the outcome.

During the fortnight, the maths department created a resource called *The Human Race – the Migrant Species*. This allowed students to examine the history of migration, not just of people throughout time but of how mathematical concepts travel from one culture to another and become assimilated into our thinking. The students were then asked to examine the following statements: 'Too many immigrants are coming into this country' and 'Our country cannot afford to help immigrants'. They used data to critically examine contentious issues and based the examinations on facts, not preconceived notions. In this example, multiculturalism and antiracist education are seamlessly embedded in a real context determined by all learners, including teachers.

In her evaluation of the fortnight, Year 9 student Louise said, 'I always thought there were lots of immigrants coming to this country, but I see that was wrong.' Students calculated that the difference immigrants make to our population is 0.03 per cent. Without helping them to develop such critical faculties however, our young people will remain susceptible to media representations of important social justice issues. To combat this, social justice teaching tries to go beyond surface presentations of issues, precisely because one way in which injustice works is by masquerading as an unchangeable *common sense* beyond the reach of critical scrutiny. Here we saw critical numeracy working on received opinions and allowing students to explore the interconnections between what they learn in school and the beliefs about what is happening in the outside world. They are moving towards a grasp of the totality, even though this process is one that never quite reaches fulfilment, as society is dynamic and understanding it can never be coterminous with it. The process allows learners to reposition themselves and base alternative decisions on their changed relationship with the world.

This work was complemented by the science department who worked on deconstructing the concept of 'race' as a non-scientific term by exploring the idea of genetic variation. This undermined the secondary school division of learning into faculty compartments. Themed learning allowed the school's specialists to work towards a rare common goal.

The English department took an empathetic approach to migration. Using photographs taken by journalist Guy Smallman, students explored the journey of a Polish migrant who is shown to be living in appalling conditions in a wood outside a small English town. Information about how immigration benefits society and the reasons why people change country was fed to the groups, who then began to try to create the story of the man in the photographs. Collating and analysing evidence and trying to begin to synthesise the material to represent the underlying moral and practical issues created a link between the lives of the learners and the realities of migration inside and outside the classroom.

This was facilitated in the next stage, when the groups were given information about shortages of workers in some of Bristol's key workplaces such as hospitals and schools. Even in the English lesson, the use of critical numeracy broke down the hermetic seals between subjects and challenged the fragmentation of knowledge characteristic of secondary schools. This is important as learners' ideas are not just shaped by the experience of these arbitrary knowledge divisions; they are further mediated by the media, which reports news in a similarly unconnected way. As a consequence of this students offered new solutions to staff shortages in different labour markets and in moving away from conventional responses, they identified barriers a migrant might have in taking up employment. Finally, students were invited to write an autobiography as if they were the man in the photograph. Constantly returning to the emotional and social consequences of migration allowed the whole person to be stimulated.

Like others before it, the project attempted to embed learning in real, often controversial issues. As Freire might have argued, here learning is contextualised or embedded in the concerns of the communities of the school. However, as this is an 'offline' simulated reproduction of reality

(Wrigley, 2006:92), a bridge is being built between everyday issues and more abstract concepts such as justice or equality. This process affords students an opportunity to reflect and allows them to reposition themselves so they can work out their own values and beliefs. During this project one Year 9 student, Tasha, commented:

> I liked learning about other people. I didn't like Polish people before – they're foreign. Now I know they're not trying to take over. I like the work we've done in English because writing about someone's life makes you realise how hard life is for immigrants. They don't just get everything they want, like benefits and a house, like we think they do.

To make projects even more real we move out of the four walls of the classroom and bring in people involved in the struggles we are exploring to talk and work with students. Previously, the school looked at climate change and had an expert witnesses' day. One of these was Elaine Graham Leigh representing the Campaign against Climate Change.

Learning also takes place offsite. During the Climate Change project in 2007, Year 9 students were offered a choice of trips: to learn how to measure a community's carbon footprint; to work with community artists to make fashion items out of 'rubbish'; or to cook in Bristol's top organic restaurant. These were a kind of community internship, however brief, where students took with them the question set by the themed learning event: how can we make the world a safer place? The theme was linked to organisations trying to solve or navigate practical solutions to climate change in the community. Again Freire's idea of *praxis* – of learning related to informed practice – is evident here.

During the cultural diversity fortnight we also decided to work with Love Music Hate Racism (LMHR). Martin Smith and Weyman Bennett, officers of Unite Against Fascism, led workshops on music and migration. On the last day LMHR put on a concert for all the school's students with *Get Cape.Wear Cape.Fly* and *Bashy*. Young people's learning is linked to their sub-cultural emotional capital. This has now become an annual event.

Tackling Islamophobia

Our latest material on *Tackling Islamophobia in secondary schools* takes this model of learning even further. One of the key challenges when delivering a cross-curricular learning project is assessment. Our learning resource is designed to challenge traditional summative assessment methods whereby progress is measured against assessment criteria and a grade or level is awarded. In place of this, students will work towards a set of values (listed below) which form the outcome, mediated and negotiated beforehand with the learners themselves.

At the start of the unit, students explore what these values mean and which of the values they consider of most importance to their own learning. This enables them each to set personalised learning targets, using the values as the basis for this. At the end of the unit students have the opportunity to reflect on how well their learning experiences have enabled them to achieve their targets.

The nine values were established by workshop participants at the *Tackling Islamophobia* conference and reflect the expertise and viewpoints of a wide range of educators. The learning intentions for each learning opportunity mirror the traditional 'learning objective': each gives a summary of the intended learning that will enable creativity in teaching practice. There are two sets of resources: one for primary and one for secondary. The secondary materials are focused on Year 9.

The Year 9 learning opportunities begin with a pair of introductory sessions in which students explore key contextual issues via a 'social simulation' and set ground rules for learning. The subsequent learning opportunities are grouped into three key curriculum areas:

- English and Media
- Art, Citizenship and PSE
- Maths, Science, MFL and PE.

The grouped learning opportunities may be taught in sequence or simultaneously across subject areas.

As the introduction says:

By the end of the learning opportunities, students will:

- be more active citizens
- be able to distinguish between discrimination and victimisation
- have explored the idea that everyone is equal and of equal value

- be able to challenge and test those beliefs which they think to be self-evident

- be able to confidently challenge Islamophobia

- want to do as they would be done by

- feel a greater sense of solidarity and community cohesion

- have established a common identity amongst themselves

- be able to evaluate the reliability and accuracy of news media and be able to recognise bias.

The learning sequence begins when Year 9 students are brought together to play a 'card game'. This simulation activity is designed to enable students to experience living in an imagined social construct inhabited by people belonging to three main age groups: 11-18, 18-34 and 35-60. Students are divided into groups and each group is given a different identity and a different set of 'life cards' depending on the group's identity. The 'life cards' represent the necessary resources (money, food and shelter), services (education, healthcare and leisure facilities) and rights (justice, freedom and equality) which enable individuals to live successfully in society. Each group's aim is to secure enough 'life cards' so that every member has one of each type and secure access to the fundamental resources, services and rights for living well. From each of the groups, one student is also selected as the *Guardian* who helps to frame the context for the simulation.

After the initial setup and introduction, the groups are given the opportunity to interact; their aim is to negotiate and trade their life cards. However, during the simulation, the Guardians will introduce a number of different scenarios which will affect the context in which students can negotiate and trade. These scenarios are designed to resemble real-life scenarios that may affect certain ethnic, religious and social groupings.

After each scenario has been played out, the Guardians will close trading and groups will be asked to reflect on their position and speculate on why they succeeded or failed to secure enough life cards for every member of the group. Finally, the debrief session allows teachers and students to explore the real-life context for the scenarios faced by groups (South Gloucestershire NUT, 2011).

After the two contextualising sessions, students and teachers can take two different routes through the lessons. One approach taken by a London secondary school suspended the curriculum for two days and taught the lessons consecutively. Here the students experienced a themed approach to the learning, one that broke down the boundaries between subjects and enhanced the process by which the developing skills and knowledge were transferred and embedded.

The underlying methodology of this approach is as important as its content. Another approach could allow for the subject areas to use the lessons provided to extend learning outwards and explore the issues in more depth. Which route is taken should ideally be decided in dialogue with the students. The redirection and refocusing of learning at the request of the learners is central to dialogic pedagogy (Freire, 1996:148-153).

The conference also wanted to support the primary classroom and materials were produced and collated for Year 4 students. The primary learning intentions of these resources are:

- to engage learners as active and expressive participants
- to raise awareness of values and perceptions
- to stimulate reactions and responses to some significant issues about Islamophobia.

The Learning Opportunities also develop a number of key skills from the primary phase including: asking and answering questions; speculation; taking on a role; exploring different interpretations of text and images; identifying an author's viewpoint; expressing personal opinions and beliefs; and the development of paired, group and class discussion skills.

At the heart of this learning sequence is a series of lessons that aim to support students in deconstructing homogeneous representations of religious and ethnic groups. For example, one lesson uses a series of fairly controversial statements like 'Chocolate is bad for you and should be banned' as a basis for getting students to practise agreeing and disagreeing in a calm and respectful manner. Based in experiences and assumptions that students can identify with, the lesson moves into more political statements like 'All Muslims are...', which allows the group to explore diversity based on their own experience.

Reconstructing pedagogies

It should be clear that these materials offer support for teachers who would like help with a challenging social justice issue such as Islamophobia. The pedagogy draws much from Freire but also from Vygotsky.

Freire was concerned to challenge the banking model of teaching in which knowledge is 'deposited' in learners' minds (Freire, 1996:53). It follows from this model that deposits have to be calculated. In most of Western education, this has meant assessment procedures fixated on measuring a learner's progress using spurious and often wholly misleading grading systems that in the context of public examinations are then subject to normative criteria after the raw scores have been produced. According to the proponents of this model of education, *assessment for learning* is merely a secondary evaluative instrument that focuses learners on outcomes rather than processes. (Even this is largely ineffective as today's C grade criteria, for example, even if mastered by the learner, may not get them a C because 'too many Cs' have been scored and normative recalculation recurs.)

Vygotsky articulated the same point: 'To implant something in the child is impossible' (van der Veer and Valsiner, 1993:331). The aim of teaching is to enable certain cognitive processes and create the conditions for learning.

Therefore any attempt to examine the teaching of social justice issues raises the dilemma of assessment. Many schools currently use a version of assessment for learning ostensibly sourced from the work of Black and William (1998). It is worth recapping the key points of this work to see how far much current practice deviates from its original aims. The pamphlet argues for:

- the provision of effective feedback to students
- the active involvement of students in their own learning
- adjusting teaching to take account of the results of assessment
- a recognition of the profound influence assessment has on the motivation and self-esteem of students, both of which are crucial influences on learning
- the need for students to be able to assess themselves and understand how to improve.

Interestingly, the group's research also indicated that teachers focussed greater 'attention on marking and grading, much of it tending to lower the self-esteem of students, rather than on providing advice for improvement' (Black and William, 1998:5).

After being formally adopted by the National Strategies in 2002, *Assessment for and of Learning* turned into a top-down procedure, in which students are shown grade criteria in order to peer- and self-assess, rather than a process in which they themselves explore collaboratively what success looks like. This has reinforced what the Assessment Reform Group thought was both a key concern and problem of much existing assessment: its fixation on grades. Such an obsession becomes demotivating for students who are unable to achieve key grades like C or a level 5.

This is a good example of how the oppressive pedagogy of teacher-led drill-test-grade now sees the child adopting the role of teacher. The learners themselves assess their work using criteria established by exam boards outside the learning context. The view that assessment could be motivating if the learner was in control of the criteria has completely vanished.

As a secondary resource, *Tackling Islamophobia in the classroom* allows students to establish the assessment criteria in the early stages of the learning journey. For instance, in the third lesson students are told that they will be assessed 'against a set of values' rather than a set of grade criteria. Nevertheless, the values are not externally set. For instance, a diamond 9 activity allows the students to determine collaboratively what those values are. This comes full circle at the end of the themed learning experience when they select evidence from the work they have completed to demonstrate success in revealing the values they identified in lesson 3. The whole process is in the hands of the learner with the teacher establishing a collaborative methodology that creates the conditions for learning.

After the initial scene-setting episodes, the lessons address how representations of Muslims affect our attitudes and opinions towards various aspects of cultural identity. In the English and media lessons students explore the complex issue of fact and opinion by analysing emotive language in tabloid newspapers. By the end of the lesson they are prepared for rewriting the story in a more positive register. From being passive consumers of certain representations of 'Muslims', students deconstruct the language and presentational devices to evaluate the decisions editors have made, and eventually become active creators of new representations.

Further lessons on challenging stereotypes follow which prepare the students for a lesson where they test out certain so-called self-evident beliefs. Teachers have expressed anxiety over such challenging moments but the ground-setting lessons forestall these concerns. The lesson begins by getting students to allocate adjectives to a series of photographs of people who they later find out are all Muslims. In one school students were surprised at the images as they did not conform to their expectations. The lesson becomes more sensitive when students look at photographs of people who died on the day of the twin towers attack and read profiles of the victims from the *New York Times*. Many students are shocked to find out that Muslims died in the towers and the lesson ends with a discussion which focuses on the following question: 'Do we expect certain behaviours from Muslims and why?'

Some teachers have reported that the power of this activity lies in students unravelling static and homogeneous representations of Muslims. This opens up a space for diverse representations of others to circulate. Others have reported that the dominant view of Muslims is so enduring that changed perceptions are only momentary.

The later Science lessons reinforce this approach. Students are buddied up with an anonymous email friend in another school and informed that they will not at first be told what the cultural identity of the person with whom they are communicating is.

Students then record a series of data about themselves from hand span to food tastes and send the information to each other. After receiving the data, students try to identify similarities and differences in the data and attempt to predict what their buddy is like. After this, groups look at 'harder' scientific data and measure such things as heart rate and reaction times after taking in caffeine. After collecting, sending and receiving the data, they set up a webcam and try to identify each other from the data they have collated.

The Maths lesson develops this theme of manipulating data to test self-evident beliefs and uses these skills to explore how data about population is represented. The learning culminates when students select evidence from the work they have completed to demonstrate success in revealing the values they identified at the beginning of the project.

This is a long way from what goes on in most secondary schools. Many have experienced difficulty in continuing the push towards themed learning even though all evaluation of the themed fortnights indicates a decrease in student discipline issues as measured by the schools' behaviour for learning policy and despite the high cognitive level of learning.

Perhaps this is why so many schools are moving to at least regular one-day themed learning events or days when the normal fare is not on offer. Another South Gloucestershire secondary, Bradley Stoke Community School, has a *Day 16*. Every sixteenth teaching day the school offers different learning experiences to the regular curriculum. Abbeywood Community School has humanities days every term.

The desire to break out of the straitjacket will increase as the move towards even more standardised testing and increasingly competitive league tables puts pressure on schools to accept the status quo, rather than take their learners on a journey that links learning to justice and to participating in transformative practices in the communities they serve. It is in this contradiction, between external government direction and the 'good sense' of schools and teachers, that a new orientation on social justice can emerge. It will be difficult. It will also become increasingly necessary if education is to become relevant to our learners and their needs.

Further reading

Tackling Islamophobia in the Classroom by Anna Brooman in Education for Liberation Journal Vol 2

INSTED website http://www.insted.co.uk/islam.html

The South Gloucestershire NUT teaching materials Tackling Islamophobia in the classroom are available at http://local.teachers.org.uk/templates/asset-relay.cfm?frmAssetFileID=9488

Acknowledgements

I would like to thank Kate Harrold and Anna Brooman for their contribution to the Tackling Islamophobia project, and especially for collecting, developing and editing the resources for primary and secondary schools respectively.

I would particularly like to thank Angus Bailey, Chris Carter, Tracey Dodds, Rachel Kendall and Laura Storey for their contribution to the Alternative Futures project at Abbeywood Community School, formerly Filton High School.

References

Abbas, T (2005) *Muslim Britain: communities under pressure.* London: Zed Books

Black, P and William, D (1998) *Inside the Black Box: raising standards through classroom assessment.* London: King's College, London, School of Education

Cantle, T (2001) *Community Cohesion: a report of the Independent Review Team.* London: Home Office

Freire, P (1996) *Pedagogy of the Oppressed.* London: Penguin

Gramsci, A (1971) *Selections from Prison Notebooks.* London: Lawrence and Wishart

Runnymede Trust (1997) *Islamophobia: a challenge for us all.* London: Runnymede Trust

Seymour, R (2010) The changing face of racism. *International Socialism* 126 p65-94

South Gloucestershire National Union of Teachers (2011) *Tackling Islamophobia in the Classroom.* Bristol: South Gloucestershire NUT website

Veer, R van der and Valsiner, J. (1993) *Understanding Vygotsky.* Oxford: Blackwell

Wrigley, T (2006) *Another School Is Possible.* London: Bookmarks

INSTED website http://www.insted.co.uk/islam.html has a range of readings about Islamophobia

9

Religion and belief: dilemmas and possibilities

Ann MacDonald

Introduction

This chapter seeks to deal not so much with the vexed question of religion(s) within the curricula and practices of schools, but rather with *faiths* as an area of concern for social justice and inclusion within schooling. The premise of this book is the right of individuals within our education systems not to experience marginalisation or exclusion. But is this right accorded to 'religious' young people? I want to suggest, with Harding (1991), that pupils who adhere to a faith tradition, be it Judaism, Islam, Christianity or any other tradition of belief, might find themselves marginalised and oppressed as a direct result of their faith, just as others do as a consequence of their gender, class, ethnicity, disability or sexuality. As teachers, we need to consider in what ways schools may be reproducing such experiences and how we might disrupt the processes which continue to exclude and to marginalise, sometimes even to demonise, particular categories of religious being. However, it may well be that such marginalisation is experienced in the context of teaching and learning in religious and moral education, and so some consideration is also given to the matter of religious education and practices within schools.

Should we have religion in schools?

The relationship between religion and schooling is emotionally and politically fraught. There are those who believe that there should be no relationship at all, that schooling should be religion-free, and that faith is a matter for individual and family life. Drawing on a major strand of the European Enlightenment tradition, some characterise religion as inherently anti-intellectual, a shackle on humanity from which we are freed through education. Thus, religion and education are conceptualised as mutually exclusive. Conversely, others point to the Establishment of the Church of England (that is, its special relationship to the state) and the Church of Scotland after the Reformation, the historical contribution of the church at the inception of free schooling (especially in Scotland, following John Knox's plea for a school in every parish), and the current legislation relating to religious observance and religious instruction in schools, to justify both the teaching and the practice of religion in schools.

What are the arguments and who is making them?

The arguments tend to be dichotomous, and often elide the complexities of the nature of religion. They tend to focus around a rebuttal of the *truth claims* of religious groups (particularly of Christianity as this has been central to the cultural production of British society) by atheist or humanist groups, often drawing on Enlightenment rationalist thinking (though the Enlightenment was less concerned to abolish religion than to place it within the limits of reason alone). In turn, church groups are keen to defend the curricular and broader social territory won for them by the historical centrality of Christian religion to culture and schooling in the UK, resisting the forces of what they see as 'secularisation' (a term to which we return later). They would argue that excluding God from schools and from the public sphere is, in a sense, itself the manifestation of a faith position, namely the belief in the absence of a deity. Further, other religious groups, understandably, want for their own faith communities the privileges they perceive Christian groups (whether Protestant or Catholic) to enjoy within schooling.

How have the arguments come about?

The background to these various positions is worth examining. Rationalist philosophy since the Enlightenment has tended to characterise faith as 'blind' and irrational. According to Rationalism, faith means believing something on the basis of authority rather than on the basis of evidence. Indeed, the European Enlightenment tradition is encapsulated in the principle that 'a wise man, therefore, proportions his belief to the evidence' (Hume, 1902:110). Religion, consequently, seems to have lost 'much of its cogency under pressure from an impersonal definition of the divine, an affirmation of the sole competence of human reason and an anthropology ill at ease with notions of human creatureliness' (Webster, 1993:209). Thus emerged the dualisms with which modernity's view of religion is imbued: faith and knowledge, real and supernatural, literal and critical, backward and progressive, bigoted and tolerant (Harding, 1991).

The response of the post Enlightenment Christian tradition was to locate faith in the 'moral sense' and in the natural orientation of humanity to God (Webster, 1993). Other major religions have responded similarly. Such rationalist thinking presupposes, however, that there is a universal Reason on which all are agreed. Yet there have been many reasons to question the idea of the sole competence of human Reason, including the philosophical doubts expressed by postmodernists, so twenty first century educational thinking in this area ought to seek a more fluid understanding.

Questions about the legitimacy of religious conviction will always exist. But it is neither possible nor appropriate in this chapter to rehearse the various ontological, cosmological or epistemological arguments for or against the existence of a deity, or deities. Even where such arguments are reviewed, it has been commonly concluded since the time of Immanuel Kant (1724-1804) that the existence of a god is neither demonstrable nor refutable by such intellectual processes (Hick, 1983). Western society has become increasingly secularised, and not just in the relative separation of church and state or in falling away of religious beliefs and practices. Over the last two centuries, we have moved from 'a society in which it was virtually impossible not to believe in God, to one in which faith, even for the staunchest believer, is one human possibility amongst others ... and in some sense an embattled option...' (Taylor, 2007:3).

How might teachers best understand the complexities of the religious identities of their pupils?

We need therefore to move away from questions about whether religions are 'real' or 'true' or about which religion, or which manifestation of any religion, is 'real' or 'true.' For the purposes of this chapter, these remain open questions. We need to move towards an understanding of religions as, at the very least, complex cultural phenomena and realise the importance of these phenomena to questions of social justice and inclusion because religious practices form a central part of the lived experience of pupils from faith traditions.

Faith may be central to the identities and identity construction of pupils from faith communities and therefore a key area in which they might experience marginalisation and the resulting barriers to participation in learning. Any assault on a pupil's faith in the context of schooling may strike at the core of their identity, and may also affect relationships between the pupil and others in their faith community, including parents.

In this chapter, I suggest that we need to reconceptualise faith and religions and the relationships they have with the social world in general. First, we need to understand religions as plural and complex, and yet interrelated. The 'religions of the Book' (Christianity, Judaism and Islam) for example share many beliefs, doctrines, prayers, rituals, and holy texts. But these faiths also have broad, shared values with other belief positions including atheism and agnosticism, since, it is argued, the sense of moral obligation (the conscience and Kant's 'Categorical Imperative') is common to all human beings (Hick, 1983). While the views of Muslims and Christians are in many respects opposed to those of, say, Marxists, an orientation towards social justice is clearly shared. Both groups can draw on the moral sources at their disposal to pledge a commitment to human rights and wellbeing and resist the consumer culture which threatens to perpetuate the marginalisation of the under-privileged (Taylor, 2007).

Second, we need to understand religions as cultural entities which are broader and deeper than adherence to a set of theological propositions. 'Religious identity is not merely defined by the cognitively drawn notion of 'belief', but more widely as 'commitment'' (Howell, 2007:373). In other words, faith might be better understood as 'commitment' rather than merely as 'belief'. Nowhere is this better demonstrated than in the Old Testament narrative of Abraham, whose terrible act of faith, when he prepared to sacrifice his only and long-awaited child on a makeshift altar, has become iconic in Judaic-Christian religious traditions. As Kierkegaard (1985) points out, it was not belief in the existence of God that was put to the test when Abraham raised his knife to his child. Rather it was his confidence not merely that *God could* restore his child, but that *God would be inclined* to restore his child to him and thus fulfil the prophecy that he would father a great nation. What was tested was his *commitment*.

Constructing religious identity narrowly as *belief*, or supposing that a repertoire of assumed truths is the central category that constitutes the religious subject, can result in an essentialising of faith which limits our understandings of the lives of people of religion (Howell, 2007). Commitment, on the other hand, 'corresponds to the lived experience ... in which 'belief' is expanded beyond the cognitive or intellectual sphere into the public realm in a way that validates and substantiates a claimed identity' (Howell, 2007:379). The self-consciously committed religious standpoint is therefore not merely a repertoire of beliefs, but a way of thinking and knowing, a way of being.

Thirdly, we need to understand religion as at once institutional and personal. The concept of *organised religion* may raise many issues of interest for social justice, not least in the areas of wealth and power. It may seem problematic that Christianity – emblematic as it is of the colonial endeavour – should produce subjects which now merit protection from the potential effects of social exclusion. Yet Harding argues that Western society has changed so significantly in relation to its religious past that Christians should be understood to occupy 'the same conceptual and political space, the vaunted margins, as women, gays, ethnic and racial minorities...' (Harding, 1991:392).

If Harding is right, the same claim could certainly be made for adherents of other, more marginalised, religions in the UK. What is important for this discussion is that, notwithstanding the reservations we may have about the institutions of organised religion, we understand the faith of pupils as authentic, whilst acknowledging the institutions of religion as bound up in hegemonic processes of power relations.

How does the marginalisation of people of faith manifest itself in schooling, and what can teachers and school leaders do about it?

I suggest three main ways in which we might recognise the marginalisation of pupils as a result of their faith or non-faith position. These suggestions are only examples, and pupils of different religious persuasions may find themselves excluded in additional ways, some of which are peculiar to their own cultural distinctions. I have termed the examples offered Christo-normativity, sectarianism and secular-normativity. Definitions and descriptions of each are offered below, along with suggestions about how they might be overcome. Each in its own way has been guilty of cultural imperialism: 'the universalisation of a dominant group's experience and culture, and its establishment as the norm...' (Young, 1990, quoted Gewirtz, 2006:74).

Christo-normativity

One common criticism of the practices associated with religion and schooling in the UK might be termed *Christo-normativity*. This can be defined as the (often subconscious) privileging of Christian beliefs and practices in the life of a school. School life lends legitimacy to Christian practices and normalises them as part and parcel of schooling in ways which potentially marginalise pupils of other faiths and those with atheist, agnostic or humanist world views. This might include termly attendance at a local Protestant church, or school assemblies presided over by the local Catholic priest. It may be manifest in the use of the Christian calendar to punctuate terms and denominate holidays. The terms Christmas and Easter, for example, refer to Christian festivals but are the words usually used to describe the winter and spring breaks. Additionally, while many schools, especially in early years departments, stage an annual nativity performance, they seldom if ever do the same for Hanukkah.

If government-funded schooling exists to serve multi-faith communities, teachers ought to reflect on the place and effects of such Christo-normative practices. We ought to examine the taken-for-granted practices we have inherited from a mono-religious past and view them through the lenses of a multi-faith society, with consideration for the multi-dimensional nature of social justice. The outcome of such reflection, however, ought not to strip schooling of all religio-cultural features. Rather we ought to engage pupils and parents in a dialogue about what is appropriate, where and for whom, and create environments which reflect and nurture the plurality of cultures and beliefs within the school community and the wider society.

One of the oft-cited defences of Christo-normative practices lies in historically situated legislation. The requirements for religious education and observance in schools vary across the UK, often for historical reasons. In some parts of the UK religious observance in schools remains a requirement of law. In Scotland, for example, following the 1872 Education Act, Religious Education was the only curriculum area required by law, and policy was set at national level; in terms of the more recent 1980 Education Act, local education authorities cannot discontinue religious observances or the provision of religious education without the approval of a majority of local electors. In England, Religious Education is compulsory but in recognition of local religious diversity, decisions about the RE curriculum are made by an advisory body under the local authority; in the case of church schools, it is the responsibility of the governing body. A 'daily act of collective worship' that is 'wholly or mainly of a broadly Christian character' is a legal requirement for all schools in England. The legal and policy landscape is shifting but principles and practices still merit examination and revision. This is all the more important in view of the fact that religious observance involves not just teaching and learning about religion(s) but also the conducting of acts of worship in and through which pupils can practice or express faith.

In theory it should not present a problem for those of a Christian persuasion to concede to the inclusion of alternative religious practices in British schools. That they do not always do so is evidence of a faith tradition which is not always faithful to itself. One of the key documents of Protestant Christianity, the Westminster Confession of Faith (1646), teaches that God alone is lord of the conscience, and lays down that worship should be initiated by the conscience of the individual rather than imposed from without. This implies the need to avoid privileging the practices of one denomination or religion over another. Further, freedom to worship (or not to worship) is seen to be a key right of the human subject as she is offered the free will to accept or reject the divine proposition.

Where there is a legal requirement or cultural expectation for acts of worship, practices vary. Some schools, especially those which serve more culturally plural communities, do attempt to provide worship contexts which are multi-faith and through which acts of religious observance can offer a meaningful reflective space for those of all faiths and none. Such attempts at ecumenism are far from straightforward, however, and raise the problem of exclusivism. The 'great world faiths' do not see each other as equally valid. Instead, at least in their orthodox manifestations, Judaism, Christianity and Islam each sees itself as the only Truth, offering the only way to God.

Even within faith traditions, there tend to be 'sibling conflict': disagreements between those of similar faith (eg. Protestants and Catholics, or Shias and Sunis) are often more bitter than those between adherents of different religions – see the section on sectarianism. Within Christianity, the Roman Catholic Church (as distinct from, say, the Church of England) sees itself as the 'one holy, Catholic church' and therefore views the rest of Christendom as errant and illegitimate. A rather different example is the resistance of many Muslims to non-Muslims teaching about their faith on their behalf, because of the risk of misrepresentation.

The problem with providing inclusive opportunities for religious observance, then, is that the synergy of faiths which is attempted through inter-faith and interdenominational practices is itself problematic – offensive even – to faith groups who understand their own position to be the only legitimate one. As those with an interest in inclusive practices in schools, we need to do better than respond to such positions by characterising them as narrow-minded or as 'bigoted'. Adherence to any faith is a complex social phenomenon and to require open-mindedness in such contexts is to entirely misunderstand and misrepresent the nature of religious identities. The requirement that faith is only to be respected where it seems to afford equal respect to other faiths and to none can lead to the perpetual exclusion and marginalisation of particular types of religious adherent. One person's bigotry is another's sincerely held religious commitment, and the name-calling only increases the polarity and perpetuates the marginalisation.

The key lies in the right of the individual pupil to worship (or not to worship) as they choose. Contexts for inter-faith religious observance should be offered, but we should understand that the individual's drive to worship in particular ways might mean that such opportunities are not taken up.

Sectarianism

Linked to this is the question of sectarianism. Sectarianism can be defined as the excessive devotion to any 'sect' or 'faction' within a religion, but in the context of the UK it is usually understood to refer to the reciprocal animosity between Protestants and Catholics and the abusive words and actions that result. It can, however, relate to other religions including Islam (between Sunni and Shia Muslims) and Judaism (between Orthodox and Reform Jews). It is now a major concern in Scotland, where the Government is urgently considering effective anti-sectarianism legislation.

The issue is enmeshed in other tensions besides those of religious division. The problem arose in the wake of the large-scale immigration of Irish workers, both Protestant and Catholic (but predominantly Catholic), to the West of Scotland in the mid nineteenth century. Protestants, many having Scottish ancestry, were more warmly received, and many immigrant Catholic families experienced victimisation and discrimination in housing and employment, and lived in severe poverty. Prior to the Education Act of 1872, education was the responsibility of the respective churches but since the 1918 Education Act Catholic children have been educated in state-funded denominational schools. This has further deepened the divide between the two traditions and lead to charges of institutional sectarianism.

Alongside this, there arose the phenomenon of secular sectarianism: Brown, for example, refers to the 'secularised nature of modern anti-catholicism' (Brown, 1987:242). Over the years Catholic immigrants set up their own cultural institutions in the face of exclusion from mainstream society. This particular variety of sectarianism is especially prominent in the rivalry between Glasgow's most famous football clubs,

Rangers and Celtic, with Protestants supporting the former and Catholics the latter. In twenty first century schools where most pupils do not claim affinity or membership of any church or religious body (and in any case both Catholic and Protestant churches do all they can to discourage sectarian hatred and violence) it is in this form of football rivalry that sectarianism often presents itself. This is perhaps further exacerbated by the influence of such bodies as the Orange Order.

In the context of schools sectarianism might occur at individual or institutional levels. Between pupils, it is likely to be manifest in name-calling, chanting, graffiti and violent abuse. But schools as institutions must ensure that they do not shore up this culture by failing to offer contexts for challenging sectarianism which involve all participants in the school community (pupils, parents, teachers, support staff and religious chaplains.) Schools often have to deal with the consequences of after-school and out-of-school behaviour as pupils from segregated schools clash on the way home. This might be a conduit for effective partnership through the use of, say, restorative practices.

The main responsibility of schools, however, is to provide effective religious education which improves mutual understanding between Protestants and Catholics and emphasises the commonalities and continuities of culture and belief. Debates about the merits and demerits of continued segregation will always be contingent on the will of powerful institutions of religion, but teachers and pupils can develop collaborative practices which might dispel conflict at local levels.

Secular-normativity

One response to the complexities of inter-religious and intra-religious tensions is to argue that schools ought to be free of religion. Accordingly, some schools have removed all religious symbols from their premises and all religious language from their documentation. Easter holidays become Spring holidays, and Christmas becomes a Winter Festival. The wearing of the hijab and the crucifix has been banned and all chaplaincies terminated. This form of militant secularism has recently developed a particular strength in France, where Muslim communities are being especially targeted. For further discussion on the growth of Islamophobia see Chapter 8.

If Christo-normativity is problematic for those of other faiths and those of none, secular-normativity is equally problematic for people of faith. Secular-normativity may be defined as privileging belief in the non-existence of a deity and the normalising of secular practices: 'the hegemony of the mainstream master narrative of secularisation' (Taylor, 2007:534). The assumption that religion has no place in schooling can lead people of faith to feel that they do not belong there either, since they are asked to leave the language and symbols of their faith at the door of the school.

If faith is a key shaper of identity, how can we promote inclusion in schools where such identities are denied legitimacy? Here, surely, is the justification for what Gewirtz, following Fraser (1997), refers to as 're-cognitional justice': the need to have one's culture recognised and respected, a condition necessary to retain dignity and self-respect (Gewirtz, 2006). There is also a very real danger that such secular-normativity will add momentum to the demand for 'faith schools' (including separate 'Christian' schools). This could increase the social tensions further.

Since the Enlightenment, people of faith have had to accept processes of accommodation into the conditions produced by the secularisation of knowledge and the 'neutralisation' of the state (Habermas and Ratzinger, 2005). Yet Christianity is holding its own, often succeeding in creating and maintaining cultural spaces which shelter it from the 'corrosive forces of modernity' (Gallagher, 2003:9). Christianity is not alone among religious persuasions in resisting extinction. Peter Thomson argues that:

> religion as both debate and way of life has not crumbled in the face of an apparently inexorable rationalist, scientific, modernising Enlightenment and the globalisation of the market economy, but retains a potency and strength which remains far in excess of its ability to explain. (Thomson, 2009:ix)

The exclusion of religion, and its associated cultures, may serve only to reduce the relevance and coherence of the school experience.

Those who argue for the secularisation of schooling appear to advocate a position of neutrality. But can this be achieved if we understand religion as something deeper and more complex than adherence to a set of beliefs, or as a set of cultural expressions? It is all too easy for such neutrality to privilege atheistic perspectives. The recent 'moral panic' around creationism in schools is one example. A small minority of pupils may come from communities which still believe the Genesis narrative should be interpreted literally. However considerably more adherents to the faiths of the Book (Judaism, Islam and Christianity) will have been taught that evolution may have been the mechanism God used to create the world. Despite this, they still believe in creation, though not in modern 'creationism'.

The insistence that creation(ism) has no place in the science classroom too easily slips into the idea of creation itself being an object of ridicule which has no legitimacy in any classroom, even the religious or philosophical one. Yet belief in a Creator is fundamental to belief in any god. How does the pupil from an orthodox Jewish tradition experience the contempt that is heaped on a narrative so central to the holy texts of his faith? What barriers does this misrecognition (Gewirtz, 2006) create for him as a learner? How are schools to negotiate this? Might open discussion about the relationship between religion, philosophy and science, and about the relative epistemologies of these disciplines, be more inclusive (and more academically robust) than a battening down of the hatches against perceived fundamentalism?

Another vexed conflict is in the area of sexuality. School communities with a commitment to social justice and inclusion are beginning to work towards practices which go further than tackling homophobic bullying by seeking to disrupt the heterosexual matrix and normalisation of heterosexuality which give rise to the marginalisation of particular categories of pupils because of their sexual orientation (DePalma and Atkinson, 2009). Attempts to adopt a culture which is genuinely inclusive of a spectrum of expressions of sexuality, however, may collide with attempts to adopt cultures which are genuinely inclusive of all faith groups. This is because the teaching of some faith groups, such as Islam, Roman Catholicism and most manifestations of Evangelical Christianity, teach that sexual relationships are legitimate only between a man and a woman, not between a man and a man or a woman and a woman (although these religious groups tend to make a distinction between homosexual orientation and homosexual practice).

The problem is indeed a perplexing one. But it is an inadequate response to suggest that sexuality is innate and religion is chosen or that the needs of those excluded on the grounds of religion must make way for the needs of those excluded on the grounds of sexuality. The provenance of both religious and sexual identities is much more complex than that. There has been an unfortunate tendency to claim that any critical comment by one group of the other is oppression or bigotry, which has resulted in discussion becoming stifled. The only possible solution seems to be a 'bottom line' one, namely the insistence that any denial of human rights on the grounds of sexuality or religion is unacceptable.

Criticism can be constructive, even desirable, however. As educators we must help learners to critique the notion that to feel offended is *de facto* to be oppressed, otherwise they will never learn tolerance, far less genuine understanding or engagement with the point of view of the other.

Perhaps the way forward lies in a deconstruction of the very binaries of the religious and the secular. The humanist argument has one key feature in common with arguments from those of various religious persuasions. It operates on the assumption that there is a clear and real difference between the religious and the secular. In a postmodern context, however, it could be argued that the terms have become unstable signifiers through which we construct the realities in which we live. The standard narrative of secularisation, whose endpoint is general indifference to religion, merits deconstruction. It might be helpful to reconceptualise secularism as not merely the absence of any religion, but as a political or intellectual standpoint that could itself be understood as a social construction.

Some scholarship problematises the status of religion in postmodernity by challenging the very categories of religious and secular, pointing to the ways in which such categories are used in strategic ways to essentialise (and sometimes marginalise) faiths by the assumed separation from the non-religious secular (Barclay, 2009). The tensions caused by conceptualising the needs of the religious and secular minorities in opposition might be broken down if we deconstruct our assumptions about the aspects of modernity we regard as religious or secular, how these differ and why this matters. The polarity of the religious and the secular might be challenged by a conceptualisation of the secular world as that which is 'characterised not by the absence of religion ... but rather by the continuing multiplication of new options, religious, spiritual, and anti-religious, which individuals and groups seize on in order to make sense of their lives...' (from the cover of Taylor, 2007). If we understand religious practices as cultural expressions, we might be less likely to discriminate against religious groups.

Summary

Even if we as educators accept the validity of an acknowledgement and exploration of religious ways of being in schooling, the way forward is far from clear. One principal issue is the extent to which one can possibly incorporate different faiths (including humanism) in the one school or education system. In the practice of the 'politics of recognition', any attempt to *include* pupils of all faiths and none quickly falls foul of the conflicting truth claims of different religions (not to mention their different metaphysical foundations), while some religious positions (such as views on sexuality) are in direct conflict with the interests of other marginalised groups. Hence we find ourselves amongst 'the lived muddle of justice ethics' (Seddon, 2003, quoted Vincent, 2003:2). This chapter has therefore attempted to highlight the fact that the aspiration to social inclusion is a complex and fraught one and that there is no set of answers or practices which we can deploy in all educational contexts for all pupils. This replicates the position of other chapters in this volume which emphasise the multi-dimensional nature of social justice, particularly its cultural and relational aspects (Gewirtz, 2006).

> ... justice can mean many things simultaneously and ... some of these things are unavoidably in tension with one another ... In practice, pursuing certain dimensions of social justice will inevitably mean neglecting, or sacrificing, others. (Gewirtz, 2006:70)

There is no given set of criteria for judging what is just. But there are recognised human rights, and these include the right (even in the school context) to practice one's religion; and the right not to be discriminated against or oppressed on the grounds of religion. In the last analysis, teachers must make these judgements for themselves on how best to facilitate this within the constraints of their local contexts. Sensitivity to the nuances to be observed across the spectrum of religious beliefs and expressions should equip educators to employ different priorities in different contexts for different purposes.

Given the deeply cultural nature of religious identity and expression and the many ways in which society is shaped and coloured by religious practices, past and present, it is difficult to envisage schooling without religion. The exclusion of religion would create a significant cultural vacuum. In reality, therefore, neither the extraction of religion from schools, nor the unquestioning practice of a particular religion in schools, is desirable or sustainable. Just as non-religious pupils may be marginalised by religious practices in schools, so might pupils from faith backgrounds be marginalised by secular-normative schooling – that is, schooling which is premised on the non-existence of a deity. What we need in schools is 'a new understanding of religious convictions as something more and something other than mere relics of a past with which we are finished' (Schuller, 2005:12). We need something more courageous than 'tolerance', more open than respect. We need genuine engagement with religions as ways of knowing and of being and as cultural expressions of humanity.

Further reading

Jackson, R (2004) *Rethinking religious education and plurality: issues in diversity and pedagogy.* Routledge Falmer, London, New York

Taylor, C (2007) *A Secular Age,* Cambridge, Massachusetts, London, Belknap Press of Harvard University Press

---

References

Barclay, F (2009) Constructing or deconstructing religion? Critical challenges to the religion industry. Unpublished paper given at conference 'What are the consequences of particular religious-secular distinctions?', 25-26 June, University of Aberdeen.

Brown, C (1987) *The Social History of Religion in Scotland since 1730.* London: Methuen

DePalma, R and Atkinson, E (ed) (2009) *Interrogating Heteronormativity in Primary Schools: the No Outsiders project.* Stoke on Trent: Trentham Books

Fraser, N (1997) *Justice interruptus: critical reflections on the 'postsocialist' condition.* New York and London: Routledge

Gallagher, S K (2003) *Evangelical Identity and Gendered Family Life.* New Brunswick, NJ: Rutgers University Press

Gewirtz, S (2006) Towards a contextualized analysis of social justice in education. *Educational Philosophy and Theory* 38(1) p69-81

Habermas J and Ratzinger, J (2005) *The Dialectics of Secularisation: on reason and religion.* San Francisco, Ignatius

Harding, S (1991) Representing fundamentalism: the problem of the repugnant cultural other. *Social Research* 58 p373-393

Hick, J H (1983) *Philosophy of Religion.* Englewood Cliffs, NJ: Prentice-Hall

Howell, B M (2007) The repugnant cultural other speaks back: Christian identity as ethnographic 'standpoint'. *Anthropological Theory* 7 p371-391

Hume, D (1902) Of miracles. In Selby-Bigge, LA (ed) *Enquiries Concerning the Human Understanding and Concerning the Principles of Morals.* Oxford: Clarenon Press

Kierkegaard, S (1985) *Fear and Trembling.* London: Penguin

Schuller, F (2005) Foreword. In Habermas, J and Ratzinger, J *The Dialectics of Secularisation: on reason and religion.* San Francisco: Ignatius

Seddon, T (2003) Framing justice: challenges for research. *Journal of Education Policy* 18(3) p229-252

Taylor, C (2007) *A Secular Age.* Cambridge, MA, and London: Belknap Press of Harvard University Press

Thomson, P (2009) Introduction: Ernst Bloch and the quantum mechanics of hope. In Bloch, E (ed) *Atheism in Christianity.* London: Verso

Vincent, C (2003) Introduction. In Vincent, C (ed) *Social Justice, Education and Identity.* London: Routledge

Webster, J B (1993) Faith. In McGrath, AE (ed) *The Blackwell Dictionary of Modern Christian Thought.* Oxford: Blackwell

Young, I M (1990) *Justice and the Politics of Difference.* Princeton, NJ: Princeton University Press

10

Rethinking poverty and social class: the teacher's response

Terry Wrigley

Forty years ago it was easy to believe that poverty belonged to the past or to distant places – images of Oliver Twist or Ethiopia would spring to mind. It was assumed that it would disappear entirely once underdeveloped countries became more modern, and that residual poverty in Britain was largely due to idleness or alcohol.

Few can still believe this in the early twenty-first century. Despite dramatic advances in productivity associated with computer technologies, and a boom time for the super-rich, child poverty statistics are scandalously high. Statistics for the UK show that child poverty more than doubled during the 1980s, and fell only slightly after 2000, when the last (Labour) government set a slow pace for its abolition. It is going up again following the financial crash (Child Poverty Action Group, c2011).

Children are more at risk than the population in general, and nearly a third of children in the UK live below the poverty line (25% in Scotland, 45% in inner London). Poverty particularly affects children in lone-parent families, largely headed by women, and those whose parents are unemployed, but not exclusively: half of the children in poverty have an employed parent, and three-fifths have two resident parents. Poverty is heavily concentrated in some big cities, but often goes unnoticed in rural areas (EKOS, 2009).

Poverty is not only inadequate food or shoes that don't fit or damp housing. It is all these things, but it is also a comparative matter, and young people become acutely aware that they cannot afford the things their friends take for granted. We know more about children's experience of poverty, from Tess Ridge's (2002) study *Childhood Poverty and Social Exclusion: from a child's perspective*. This research revealed that:

- poorer children are unlikely to receive regular pocket money, and this restricts their independence
- not being able to afford transport affects their opportunity to sustain friendships
- not having the right clothing affects relationships and self-esteem, and can lead to bullying
- being unable to afford school trips affects relationships with peers and teachers, as well as damaging learning
- children have to reject friends' invitations to join them in weekend activities.

Fears of loneliness and isolation are very real, and acutely felt:

> Couldn't do nothing on the weekends, just stayed in, couldn't go out with my friends and go to the shop or anything like that, so ... bit boring. (Ridge, 2006: 26)

Children growing up in poverty often moderate their requests, deny their needs and wants, and self-exclude from school trips to protect their parents' feelings:

> It was real hard ... 'cos all our mates would be doing everything and we'd think – 'oh I want to do that'. We'd try and ask mum, but then we'd think, what if she says, 'well look I've only got a bit of money', then we'd feel guilty for asking, so we didn't ask her. (Ridge, 2006:26)

Living in a consumer society increases the damage and sense of losing out. It affects confidence, social development and self-esteem:

> If you don't wear trendy stuff ... not so many people will be your friend 'cos of what you wear. (Charlene, 12 years, two-parent family)

> I can't go out and look scruffy or anything like that. I won't go out if I look scruffy, I won't do it. (Colleen, 13 years, lone-parent family) (Ridge, 2002:68-70)

Poverty often involves living in more troubled parts of cities, and children have to learn the skills to deal with this:

> You just like walk past them, don't even look at them, you don't look back if they say anything. [Then] usually they leave you alone. (11-year-old boy) (Hill *et al*, 2006:46)

Young people learn to move about in a group to become more safe, but may be seen as threatening by adults as a result. Many face the disruption of having to move house and school, which impacts on relationships, confidence and aspirations.

A lot of stigma is attached to poverty, which particularly affects young people while they are developing identities. This can have a serious impact on school learning and aspirations.

Poverty affects people both materially and in their relationships, and has a symbolic impact in addition. It is naïve to ascribe it to individual laziness for several reasons: many graduates can't find work; people doing less skilled jobs often have to accept flexible contracts with unreliable and variable hours, and their rates of pay are insufficient to keep a family. Those without work, including mothers with young children or disabled people, are routinely vilified by politicians and newspapers who deem them 'benefit scroungers'.

Understanding poverty and class

It is important to clarify the terms used when discussing poverty and class and understand the connection between these concepts.

Firstly, we can distinguish between *absolute* and *relative* poverty. Absolute poverty is most widespread in poorer, less industrialised countries, but has not disappeared here. Its impact includes children going to school without breakfast, having no hot meals during school holidays, sleeping in damp or cold rooms, and being prone to respiratory diseases. Absolute poverty signifies the inability to maintain your body in reasonable health.

A much larger group of people live in relative poverty. This concept refers to a sense of deprivation relative to current social expectations and includes not being able to do the things considered normal – such as wear the right clothes, go on school trips, go to the swimming baths or have a family holiday. It is measured, for convenience, according to how far your income is below average (generally 50% or 60% of average income, adjusted for the number of family members and sometimes housing costs). Children who experience absolute poverty also suffer relative poverty.

Class is an even more complex idea, and terms such as *working class* and *middle class* take on varying meanings which we need to disentangle. Traditionally, the term *working class* applies to manual workers, and middle class to people working in offices or shops or professions such as teaching. This is extremely problematic as a division.

A good starting point for breaking down this association is Marx's (1848) argument that (even then) society was dividing more and more into two major classes:

> those who 'own the means of production', ie, the wealthy who own land, mines and factories
>
> workers for wages who have 'only their labour power to sell' and need to work for the first group or else starve.

In these terms, not only manual workers but also 'middle-class' secretaries, nurses and teachers belong to the second group – employees. (There are many self-employed people who don't fit into either category, but in Marx's terms the self-employed do not constitute a class because they can't organise together as an independent power in society and therefore do not collectively affect the flow of history.)

Under Marx's definition, most people suffering from poverty are part of a broader working class which includes not only industrial workers and road diggers but also nurses, classroom assistants and teachers. Most people in poverty are either working, generally in part-time or low-paid jobs, or, if unemployed, are looking for work or have a disability. They are a section of this large working class who, for various reasons, are more vulnerable than most.

Some workers are more likely than others to be affected since poverty intersects with other inequalities. Despite legislation, racial prejudice still makes it harder to get decently-paid employment, and refugees are made particularly vulnerable. This is clearly visible in London, where low-paid office cleaners for example are overwhelmingly darker skinned. Mothers of young children often encounter prejudice in the form of employers' or managers' assumptions that they will prove unreliable because of childcare needs. They are additionally disadvantaged by working in part-time jobs which are often paid less per hour. People with disabilities face difficulties securing jobs which they could do well if only employers would make basic adjustments.

But ethnicity, gender and disability are not the root causes. Applicants for jobs can be rejected for being either too old or too young. You can be turned down for not having the experience, so you don't get the chance to gain the experience. Some employers eliminate applicants in the wrong postcode because of the stigma attached to living in poorer neighbourhoods. People who, for whatever reason, have limited school qualifications are not shortlisted for jobs which they could do perfectly well; the formal qualifications become an arbitrary gatekeeper unrelated to the skills required for the work. Many young graduates are employed in low-paid unreliable work, in places like call centres for example. Manual workers with years of experience in mining, shipbuilding, steelmaking, car manufacture and other industries have ended up in long-term unemployment or poorly paid 'service work' when their workplaces were closed down or moved overseas. At the heart of the problem is not the characteristic of the worker, but an economic and political system which fails to utilise the skills of so many people, and where the few make vast fortunes from the low pay of the many.

Recognising that people in poverty are part of a (broadly defined) working class leaves two major problems however. Firstly, since the 1980s it has become common to label people in poverty as an *underclass*, a pejorative term. American academic Charles Murray (1990) popularised this expression, claiming that inner cities and council estates are full of work-shy people who prefer a life of crime or, in the case of women, have children in order to live off benefits. Valuable counter-evidence can be found in research by Robert MacDonald and Jane Marsh which focused on one of the poorest estates in Britain, on Teesside. Through numerous interviews, MacDonald and Marsh (2005) showed that despite high unemployment, these young people still want to work, settle down and raise a family. Most move between spells of unemployment and periods of 'poor work', ie low-paid, insecure jobs with irregular hours. The other groups strongly affected by this kind of employment are refugees, asylum seekers and other migrants (Sivanandan, 1989).

The second problem, for teachers in particular, relates to the division between so-called working-class (ie manual) and middle-class (ie non-manual) occupations. Although there is no fundamental difference between these two sets of workers, it has been evident for many years that, even when they attend the same school, there is a general tendency for children of white-collar or professional parents to achieve more than those of manual workers. (Please note: a *tendency* does not mean this is true of everyone, or even of most people in each group.)

Many possible explanations can account for this: family conversation in many professional and other white-collar households may come closer to the academic language used in school, parents in these families have a clearer understanding of what schools and universities expect, and friends of their families may serve as role models for careers which depend on academic success. There is also a connection with parents' own levels of education: 'middle-class' parents have generally been educated for longer and since many have university degrees they often expect their children to acquire the same – see the explanation of cultural capital below.

Many of these arguments are problematic and unresolved. So when we look at why some children, including those who become disaffected, are having little success at school, we may be looking at a complex mix of the impact of absolute poverty, relative poverty, and parents working in low skilled occupations and having lower levels of education. The mix will vary in each case: some children in poverty are being brought up by a university-educated single mother who is temporarily unable to work; others with less educated parents have grandparents or neighbours who are able to stimulate and help with schoolwork and so on.

Poverty and schooling

Britain has one of the highest levels of child poverty in Europe and the PISA international tests show that the impact of poverty on school achievement is also quite high (OECD, 2010b). This implies the need not only for government policies to lift people out of poverty but also for teachers to be proactive in raising questions about how schools can help. We are dealing with a highly complex problem which offers no easy answer and unless teachers become informed about the issues at hand, they may offer inadequate responses which can make matters worse.

Problems arise in particular from adopting derogatory and deficit views of people or generalising to assume that everybody is affected by the same issues. Either of these leads to defeatism and a reinforcement of deficit understandings.

Poverty is correlated with underachievement from a very early age. Whilst it is difficult to assess 3 to 5 year-olds, if we take vocabulary acquisition and simple problem-solving into account, an impact is already demonstrable by the age of 3 (Bradshaw, 2011). It is important to recognise however that this is a statement about *averages*: once we start to think of all children in poverty as having low achievement or a poor start in life, it becomes easy to lower expectations and teach down to that level. Part of this variability is due to different levels of parental education: a third of mothers in the poorest fifth of families have Highers, A-levels or degrees, for example.

Good nursery education, as well as stimulation from parents, makes a difference but here too, generalisations can lead teachers to stereotype poorer families. Though it is true that parents who are better-off (and tend to be better educated) read to their children more often, this doesn't imply that poorer parents don't. Recent research for the Scottish Government (Bromley, 2009) shows that 78 per cent of the richest fifth look at books with their 1 and 2 year-old children every day, but so do 55 per cent of the poorest fifth. Surprisingly, the figures are quite similar when comparing mothers over 40 and below 20, and when comparing mothers with degrees to those with no qualifications.

So while it is valid to emphasise the importance of nursery education and recognise that children growing up in some families start off at a disadvantage, we mustn't underestimate or write off children who are growing up in poverty.

Unfortunately, there is clear research which shows that the achievement gap widens as children proceed through school. While there are good explanations as to why this should be, including an increasing sense of alienation during the teenage years we should not dismiss the possibility that schools and teachers have an important role to play in reducing poverty-related underachievement.

Whatever the combination of economic, home and school factors, the data is challenging. While in primary school, the highest-achieving pre-school children from poorer families are overtaken by the lowest-achieving children of richer families. Among children on free school meals, a minority end primary school in the top fifth of the population by attainment, but then there is a further drop-out: only one in seven of these children who achieve highly at age 11 despite poverty subsequently reaches university (Sutton Trust, 2008).

False trails and half truths

It is important to understand some historic explanations of the link between poverty and low achievement since they continue to have an impact today. Until the twentieth century, the dominant view in England was that that low educational achievement for poorer working-class children was right and fitting: schools should *fit* people for their *place* in society and not lead to false expectations. A more democratic belief in Scotland held that everybody should be literate enough to read the Bible and to this was added a belief in supporting talented individuals from poorer families. This was symbolised by the notion of the 'lad o' pairts', which asserted that even though a person might come from humble beginnings, with hard work and merit they can achieve – David Livingstone is probably the most famous example. Bursaries were established for poor boys and girls to go to university. The school system in Scotland gave a direct route from the parish school to university, unlike England with its exclusive grammar and private schools which led to Oxford and Cambridge. However, even in Scotland the majority of poorer children had a limited, short and harsh experience of education.

In the twentieth century, with the rise of trade unions and the foundation of the Labour Party, workers would no longer tolerate their children being written off like this. The ruling class soon adopted a different discourse, based on the belief that children had a fixed level of 'intelligence' which was inherited to a large degree from their parents (see Cowburn, 1986). Tests were developed which claimed to measure innate intelligence rather than what children had learned at home or school, though how they could separate these factors was never explained.

Not surprisingly, the children of better-off and generally better-educated parents performed better in these tests. It was just as logical to see this as the result of differences in environment as of differences in inherited ability, but the latter conclusion was ideologically convenient to the upper classes who wished to justify their own higher status.

The terrible loss of life and talent in the First World War then created an economic need to improve the education and skills of the most promising working-class children. Free secondary education was provided for high-achieving working-class children who passed the scholarship exam at 11, though many – including my own parents – couldn't take advantage of it as they were unable to even afford the school uniform.

Many doubts remained about the belief in a unified generic intelligence and the mechanisms used for testing it. An alternative model suggested that 'intelligence', as a set of problem-solving capacities, is not a single item but a variety of abilities, each related to different activities which partially overlap. The empirical data supports either model – see Gould 1996 for a detailed explanation. The discovery that the measured 'intelligence' of particular populations (eg. Italian migrants to the USA or conscripts to the armed forces) improved from one decade to another contradicted its supposed innateness.

How could it be claimed that intelligence tests measured how much intelligence you were born with when you could improve your scores through practice? During the 1950s and 60s, when children's access to a decent secondary education depended on a test of supposedly innate intelligence, upper primary children typically spent an hour a day practising the tests to raise their scores! Some lower-level secondary schools successfully entered 16-year-olds who had failed the test for exams intended for those who had passed (Chitty, 2009:85). Finally, key research by Cyril Burt based on identical twins who had been separated through adoption and supposedly proving that they retained the identical levels of intelligence passed on through their genes, turned out to be fraudulent (Hearnshaw, 1979). By the 1960s the edifice collapsed.

There followed a dramatic shift towards explanations based on early childhood upbringing and the influence of parents and neighbours. In the USA, the key arguments were racial: African Americans supposedly did worse at school because their dialect was illogical; they used double negatives such as 'We ain't got none', for example. (The researchers didn't seem to realise that this features in French and many other languages.) This provided an excuse not to improve the very poor spending on African Americans' schools.

The major argument in Britain (Bernstein, 1971) was rather more sophisticated, namely that working-class (ie manual worker) families tended to talk about things which were immediately visible and used a 'restricted code' which preferred pronouns to nouns. Again this was based on flawed research: when describing what they saw in a cartoon, the working-class children very sensibly used pronouns because the picture story was in front of them. This was actually more appropriate than the 'middle-class' children's use of nouns, but presumably the latter had a sense of which style academic researchers might prefer.

The notion of a 'restricted code' among manual-worker families quickly led to a professional mythology which was deeply prejudiced. It became common for teachers to explain that 'working-class children don't do well at school because their parents smack them instead of talking to them'. (Ironically, at that time, children were regularly subject to painful physical punishment at school.) This excused the profession from asking questions about the different styles of teaching which different children were exposed to.

Around the same time, Barnes (1969) and others demonstrated that much of the language usage in schools was seriously restricted. Perhaps this occurs most of all in schools which serve poorer neighbourhoods. The predominance of closed questions restricts pupils to factual answers, based on memory rather than reasoning; and the style and frequency of questions intended to test rather than explore or challenge makes it almost impossible to give an answer of more than three words. Others (Labov, 1969; Rosen, 1972) argued that people could use various styles of language to pursue serious thoughts, and that many working-class communities were characterised by industrial struggle and radical politics where people regularly discuss 'distant' and serious issues such as why they are poorly paid or why the country was going to war.

Both these arguments, of fixed innate intelligence and of a 'restricted code' of language use, may seem outdated but in variant forms they have ongoing effects. Consider assumptions that children in poverty have never seen a book and don't know which end to start at – in reality their mothers may be passing on a fear of damaging library books because they can't afford to replace them. We should also consider the implications of P1 (Y1) teachers placing pupils on different tables according to 'ability'. What do they mean by *ability*? Is this an implicit belief that children have different quantities of innate intelligence? Do teachers sufficiently consider that some children have had a quite different range of early experiences, or that those who have been to museums and watched nature programmes on TV engage more confidently with their teachers and give them the impression of higher intelligence? Do secondary teachers examine whether some of the pupils in their class lack the prior experiences they might need to understand their teacher's' abstract language, whether speaking about medieval monasteries or the solar system?

Expectations and aspirations

A frequent explanation of underachievement is the low aspirations of parents and children, or the suggestion that they don't care about their future. It is important to examine this argument critically.

We should understand how it arises out of experiences. Teachers staying late for parents evening, frustrated by the absence of certain families, easily assume that the parents 'couldn't care less'. There may be all sorts of reasons, including irregular working hours, the need to look after other children or feelings of anxiety or antipathy towards school – a legacy of their own negative experiences of schooling. Some schools are more successful than others in maintaining contact and include conversations with parents in the playground and informal consultations in the classroom at the end of the day as well as initiating contact by phone. While some parents are harder to reach than others, we also need to recognise that some schools are less welcoming than others and take fewer initiatives to get parents involved.

A recent research report on white working-class families in London (Demie and Lewis, 2010:251) includes the following quotations from heads and teachers:

> Many are young single mothers who had a negative experience of school and became pregnant soon after leaving school, as did their mothers, they follow the pattern ... Many have never worked; they ... *do not want to work.* (School A)

> They are *settling for* scraping by each week. I *see* mothers outside the school gate with their own mothers *having the attitude, I'm ok, I'll just do what my mum does.* (School G) (my italics)

The researchers took these assertions at face value, rather than raising critical questions. They might have asked whose perspective this is written from and what is the evidence. What do the speakers really know about the lives, thoughts and motivations of these mothers? The perspective is that of the all-knowing professional staring out from the school window onto distant mothers who are kept on the margins of the school, understanding their attitudes and view of life through some kind of intuition or telepathy. Such a perspective fails to recognise that aspirations depend substantially on what people sense are realistic options. Aspirations depend on opportunities; they are not simply a product of personal optimism.

This partly depends on location: towns which have experienced the closure of major industries and high levels of unemployment are not exactly places where people develop ambitions, as we see from these extracts from interviews with people in the former mining and steel towns of South Yorkshire illustrate:

> I've done nothing but be unemployed. Life ended when I finished in the pit and it hasn't ever started again. All there's been is this nothingness. My life stopped.

> We were the lost children of Thatcher's government ... If they could have, they'd have gassed us like they did in Germany, because we were neither use nor ornament. (Charlesworth, 2000:93-4, rewritten without local dialect)

People learn a fatalistic coping in these environments, and high aspirations are the exception rather than the norm. A common and shared experience of closed doors, dead ends and limited prospects (Bourdieu, 1977:86) naturally affects attitudes to education, especially when it is

156

perceived that qualifications and training don't necessarily lead to well-paid work.

This combines with parents' experiences of school which has often involved a lack of respect, and low-level tedious learning tasks:

> They're not bothered. There's no point. When you go to them anyway, they talk to you like you're not there. Most of the time they don't even wanna know yer. And when they do it's only to shout at you or something, and put you down. (interview in Charlesworth, 2000:127)

This realisation can lead to the wrong conclusions. Arguments have been made that a 'culture of poverty' exists among an 'underclass' who supposedly prefer crime and benefits to work. Such arguments have a long history and can become part of the narrative of government. The chancellor of the exchequer George Osborne – who is a multi-millionaire – speaks of life on unemployment benefits as a 'lifestyle choice' (*Guardian*, 9.9.2010). MacDonald and Marsh's research (eg. 2005) shows that even in areas of high unemployment, people still hold on to a belief in the importance of work and the desire to look after a family well, and employ complex strategies to maintain self-respect in difficult environments.

As educators, we should also recognise the impact of media disparagement of families and indeed whole neighbourhoods living in poverty. This is something which inevitably spreads to teachers: a single encounter with an angry mother can quickly lead us to make negative generalisations about an entire housing scheme. Teachers are not immune from the insulting stereotypes presented by sensationalist newspapers and television documentaries – see the powerful treatment of this issue in Owen Jones's 2011 book *Chavs: the demonisation of the working class*.

This should not lead teachers to a sense of despair but to a determination to challenge the situation on many fronts. Schools can play a part by creating a positive climate based on respect for children and parents. They can offer a space where parents are made welcome and appreciative discussions about children's difficulties and development can take place between parents and teachers. Too much school work has an audience of one – the teacher with her marking pen. In neighbourhoods where opportunities are bleak it is particularly important to show that pupils' school work is highly valued – not just through praise, but by display, reading work aloud, performance and presentation (see numerous examples in Wrigley, 2000).

The meaning of culture

Culture doesn't just mean paintings and books – it is a whole way of life. The habits and norms of schools, including an emphasis on display and performances, are part of the school's culture.

Teachers and school leaders concerned about child poverty need to reflect carefully on the culture of their particular school. This should be part of the collective process of school self-evaluation, one which asks questions about the messages and beliefs carried by physical environment, ways of talking with children and seating arrangements, as well as curriculum, assessment and teaching styles. In *Schools of Hope* (2003) I made the following suggestions for such a self-evaluation of school culture:

- examining the cultural messages of classrooms which are dominated by the teacher's voice, closed questions and rituals of transmission of superior wisdom
- developing a better understanding of cultural difference, in order to prevent high levels of exclusion
- understanding how assumptions about ability and intelligence are worked out in classroom interactions
- discovering how assumptions about single parents, ethnic minorities and 'dysfunctional' working-class families operate symbolically in classroom interactions. (Wrigley, 2003:36-37)

These suggestions are particularly significant in relation to children growing up in poverty. Placing 6 year-olds on the tortoise table (children are quick to see through our ingenious codes) impacts on their self-belief and future progress. It also intersects with other dimensions of inequality; the child in poverty who is also from a home where English is not spoken is easy to label 'backward'. Why is it still common to hear derogatory remarks about single mothers with reference to the pupils' parents, when teachers who are single mothers are spoken of with admiration and respect? Habitual ways of speaking about children and families in the staffroom inevitably leak through into ways we treat children in class.

One helpful theoretical treatment of culture is Bourdieu's concept of *cultural capital* (Bourdieu and Passeron, 1977). He argues that powerful social institutions such as schools tend to recognise some forms of cultural activity and ignore or belittle others. To give a crude example, a high school pupil having cello lessons might be assumed to be cultured, intelligent and from a 'good family', whereas if another pupil has learned bass guitar from his dad, the teachers probably don't even know – if they do they might even fulminate about the immoral lifestyle of heavy metal bands.

It is important not to misunderstand Bourdieu. He is not suggesting that some sections of society are *more* cultured than others, though it is true that money affects the opportunity to pursue cultural interests. His argument is one of recognition and misrecognition, of what matters to schools. He uses the word *capital* as a metaphor, using the analogy of rich people having financial capital they can invest, because esteemed cultural attributes – be they the clothes we wear, the books we read, or the qualifications we hold – help give access to better careers and financial prosperity.

This raises some important questions about what schools recognise and misrecognise, and there have been valuable attempts to include learning practices in schools which respect and build upon community-based knowledge. Moll and Greenberg (1990) explored how skills are shared among immigrant Mexican families in the USA and worked with teachers to draw on that knowledge. Pat Thomson (2006) provides examples from Australia of how school-community projects can draw on pupils' hidden knowledge; she refers to this as a 'virtual schoolbag'. This is far more productive than thinking of the local neighbourhood as a bundle of problems.

So what can be done?

Schools can make a difference, but not *all* the difference (Mortimore and Whitty, 1997). We need to be honest and recognise that underachievement can never be adequately dealt with while child poverty continues. Many teachers in poorer neighbourhoods have become involved in local political struggles beyond the school gate to make life better, for example putting pressure on the council to improve housing or to reduce racism in an area.

There are some issues which clearly require a response beyond the classroom. For example, it is likely that our current way of organising S1-2 (Y7-8) classes, with pupils facing over a dozen teachers a week, makes it difficult for supportive relationships to develop; to change this by having some teachers covering more than one subject requires a policy decision.

Research shows that the best early years provision involves children's centres which welcome parents to participate in activities so that approaches to playing and talking with children can be shared and improved (Sylva *et al*, 2004); such centres include book and toy libraries and the availability of advice from health professionals. This also requires decisions by the local authority, so concerned teachers need to find ways of influencing local policy-makers.

Some changes need decisions at whole-school level. Practices such as taking groups of secondary pupils to visit universities, or bringing former pupils as role models to a school, need the collective decision or at least approval of staff to succeed.

There are other matters which teachers can change in their everyday classroom work, though this is more effective when two or three are collaborating; this way individuals avoid being isolated and can begin to have an influence on the rest of the school. A small group of committed teachers can engage in peer observation and joint planning, and find occasions for showing the results to other pupils and staff. Similarly, residentials for curriculum enhancement or visits to historic sites can only become standard practice if there is a weight of staff approval.

Though there has been little formal research in Britain on the 'pedagogy of poverty' (Haberman, 1999), it is easy to observe how pupils in poorer neighbourhoods, and particularly in lower streams and sets, are constantly subjected to low-challenge routine tasks – in effect, a debased curriculum. One of the most important challenges for teachers is to introduce high-challenge engaging tasks which are accessible to pupils with less developed core skills; basic skills of literacy or ICT need to be embedded into interesting activities rather than endless decontextualised exercises. This is true at every stage: whatever the benefits of a particular technique – synthetic phonics, for example – literacy cannot be regarded as a set of routine 'skills'. As Jim Cummins argues with regard to many phonics programmes,

> Nowhere in this anemic instructional vision is there room for really connect-
> ing at a human level with culturally diverse students; consigned to irrelevance
> also is any notion of affirming students' identities, and challenging coercive
> power structures, by activating what they already know about the world and
> mobilising the intellectual and linguistic tools they use to make sense of their
> worlds. This kind of programming reduces instruction to a technical exercise.
> No role is envisaged for teachers or students to invest their identities (affect,
> intellect and imagination) in the teaching/learning process ...
>
> When we frame the universe of discourse only in terms of children's deficits
> in English and in phonological awareness (or deficits in any other area), we
> expel culture, language, identity, intellect, and imagination from our image of
> the child ... In contrast ... an instructional focus on empowerment, understood
> as the collaborative creation of power, starts by acknowledging the cultural,
> linguistic, imaginative, and intellectual resources that children bring to
> school. (Cummins, 2003:56-57)

Some change in classroom practice requires a rethinking of patterns which are normally taken for granted or 'below the radar'. For example, why do we assume that maths is more connected with physical manoeuvres such as emptying and filling baths than with real-world problems such as divisions of wealth and poverty or the environment? Why is it that school learning so rarely ends in a display or presentation, whether to other students or a wider audience? Why does 'problem-solving' rarely involve real-life problems? Many of these issues are tackled in the Australian *productive pedagogies* project (Hayes *et al*, 2006).

Even in neighbourhoods damaged by poverty, teachers are, understandably, nervous about bringing it into the curriculum. And when they do the pupils' voices are missing, so that it ends up with moralistic advice on alcohol abuse, unhealthy diets and early pregnancy, underpinned by implicit deficit views of the local area and families. Yet young people are not served by excluding their lives and circumstances from the curriculum. They have a right, as citizens, to honest discussion about why society is so unequal and how they can change it.

These are fundamental and challenging questions, which require teachers to engage not only as individuals within classrooms, but with groups of colleagues, and networking beyond the school, as well as engaging with the wider community to inform and influence policymakers.

Further reading

Smyth, J and McInerney, P (2007) *Teachers in the middle: reclaiming the wasteland of the adolescent years of schooling* (Peter Lang)

Smyth, J and Wrigley, T (2013) *Living on the edge: re-thinking poverty, class and schooling* (Peter Lang)

Wrigley, T, Thomson, P and Lingard, B (eds 2012) *Changing schools: alternative ways to make a world of difference* (Routledge)

References

Barnes, D (1969) Language in the secondary classroom. In Barnes, D, Britton, J and Rosen, H and the L.A.T.E *Language, the Learner and the School.* Harmondsworth: Penguin

Bernstein, B (1971) *Class, Codes and Control 1: theoretical studies towards a sociology of language.* London: Routledge and Kegan Paul

Bourdieu, P and Passeron, J-C (1977) *Reproduction in Education, Society and Culture.* London: Sage

Bradshaw, P (2011) *Growing up in Scotland: changes in child cognitive ability in the pre-school years.* Edinburgh: Scottish Government

Bromley, C (2009) *Growing up in Scotland: the impact of children's early activities on cognitive development.* Edinburgh: Scottish Government

Charlesworth, S (2000) *A Phenomenology of Working Class Experience.* Cambridge: Cambridge University Press

Child Poverty Action Group (c2011) *Poverty in the UK: a summary of facts and figures,* http://www.cpag.org.uk/povertyfacts (accessed Nov 2011)

Chitty, C (2009) *Eugenics, Race and Intelligence in Education.* London: Continuum

Cowburn, W (1986) *Class, Ideology and Community Education.* London: Croom Helm

Cummins, J (2003) Challenging the construction of difference as deficit: where are identity, intellect, imagination, and power in the new regime of truth? In Trifonas, P (ed) *Pedagogies of Difference: rethinking education for social change.* London: RoutledgeFalmer

Demie, F and Lewis, K (2010) White working class achievement: an ethnographic study of barriers to learning in schools. *Educational Studies* 37(3)

EKOS (2009) *The Experience of Rural Poverty in Scotland.* Edinburgh: Scottish Government Social Research

Gould, S (1996) *The Mismeasure of Man.* New York: W W Norton

Haberman, M (1999) *Star Principals: serving children in poverty.* Indianapolis: Kappa Delta Pi

Hayes, D, Mills, M, Christie, P and Lingard, B (2006) *Teachers and Schooling Making a Difference: productive pedagogies, assessment and performance.* Crows Nest: Allen and Unwin

Hearnshaw, L (1979) *Cyril Burt, Psychologist.* London: Hodder and Stoughton

Hill, M, Turner, K, Walker, M, Stafford, A and Seaman, P (2006) Children's perspectives on social exclusion and resilience in disadvantaged urban communities. In Tisdall, E Kay M, Davis, J, Hill, M and Prout, A (ed) *Children, Young People and Social Inclusion: participation for what?* Bristol: Policy Press

Jones, O (2011) *Chavs: the demonization of the working class*. London: Verso

Labov, W (1969) The Logic of Nonstandard English. *Georgetown Monographs on Language and Linguistics,* vol 22

MacDonald, R and Marsh, J (2005) *Disconnected Youth? Growing up in Britain's poor neighbourhoods*. Basingstoke: Palgrave Macmillan

Marx, K and Engels, F (1996/1848) *The Communist Manifesto*. London: Phoenix

Moll, L and Greenberg, J (1990) Creating zones of possibilities: combining social contexts for instruction. In Moll, L (ed) *Vygotsky and Education: instructional implications and applications of sociohistorical psychology*. Cambridge: Cambridge University Press

Mortimore, P and Whitty, G (1997) *Can School Improvement Overcome the Effects of Disadvantage?* London: Institute of Education

Murray, C (1990) *The Emerging British Underclass*. London: Institute of Economic Affairs

OECD (2010b) PISA 2009 at a Glance. OECD Publishing; http://dx.doi.org/10.1787/97892 64095298-en (accessed 4 Feb 2012)

Ridge, T (2002) *Childhood Poverty and Social Exclusion: from a child's perspective*. Bristol: Policy Press

Ridge, T (2006) Childhood poverty: a barrier to social participation and inclusion. In Tisdall, E Kay M, Davis, J, Hill, M and Prout, A (ed) *Children, Young People and Social Inclusion: participation for what?* Bristol: Policy Press

Rosen, H (1972) *Language and Class: a critical look at the theories of Basil Bernstein*. Bristol: Falling Wall Press

Sivanandan, A (1989) New circuits of imperialism. *Race and Class* 30 p1-19

Sutton Trust (2008) *Wasted Talent? attrition rates of high-achieving pupils between school and university,* www.suttontrust.com

Sylva, K, Melhuish, E, Sammons, P, Siraj-Blatchford, I and Taggart, B (2004) *The Effective Provision of Pre-school Education (EPPE) Project. Final report*. London: DfES/Institute of Education, University of London

Thomson, P (2006) Miners, diggers, ferals and show-men: school-community projects that affirm and unsettle identities and place? *British Journal of Sociology of Education* 27(1) p81-96

Wrigley, T (2000) *The Power to Learn: stories of success in the education of Asian and other bilingual pupils*. Stoke on Trent: Trentham Books

Wrigley, T (2003) *Schools of Hope: a new agenda for school improvement*. Stoke on Trent: Trentham Books

11

'Not much I can do – he's got ADHD'

Gwynedd Lloyd

This chapter takes a look at what we mean by Attention Deficit Hyperactivity Disorder (ADHD) and asks how and why it has apparently become so widespread across the world in the last fifteen years. When you think about ADHD there are a number of questions you should consider. How do we describe it? Why has it become so widespread? Where did it come from? Is it a 'disease' of particular cultures? Does it require very distinctive interventions from specialist professionals? Is pharmaceutical treatment the best remedy? What can teachers do? How can we support and include without labelling in a way that limits students' personal and educational possibilities?

While I am critical of the concept of ADHD as a psychiatric diagnosis, I do not deny that there are students in schools and children in families who present and experience real difficulties. So in this chapter I try to present a view that is critical of the assumptions and practices that lead to such increased numbers of children receiving the diagnosis of ADHD and associated medication, but also to offer some help and advice to teachers and other professionals working with children and young people with difficulties of this kind.

Simon Bailey (2009) writes interestingly of the possibilities of taking a critical view while acknowledging the difficulties faced by some young people, rejecting a binary view of ADHD as either a myth or a clear measurable reality. He describes his own diagnosis of ADHD, arguing that there is:

> a certain reality of ADHD I accept within my own identity. A reality I can see as having had an impact on my experience of life and a reality that impairs me still. On the other hand I remain critical of it as a construct. I do not believe that it has any particular explanatory power and I find it offensive when others use it as an explanation of my actions ... One of the consequences of gathering together a set of individual deficits and giving them a name has been to make me focus on these deficits. (Bailey, 2009:18)

This view incorporates an acknowledgement of some of his own characteristics but also a reluctance either to be defined by this, as a cluster of deficits, or to see his behaviour as determined by them, apparently limiting the possibility of making his own choices about his actions. Many parents and teachers may see an ADHD diagnosis as the way to obtain professional help, but it can label children negatively as an 'ADHD child' or 'ADHD pupil' and limit the ways in which children and young people think they can construct their own lives. The label can also make teachers and other educational professionals worry that they need special techniques to include and support these pupils. Vallee, discussing ADHD, recognises that 'western, as well as non-western, illness categories are culture bound' and argues for an 'elucidation of diagnostic and treatment implications associated with adopting a reductionistic diagnostic approach' (Vallee, 2011:85).

What is ADHD?

ADHD is a professional label, a medical diagnosis that comes from the American Psychiatric Association's Diagnostic and Statistical Manual. Like many such labels, it began life as a 'syndrome', or a loose collection of behaviours which appeared somehow linked, before it took on a life of its own. The Manual, which is revised every few years, gives a descriptive guide to the behaviour associated with a range of psychiatric 'disorders'. The Manual changes to some extent with each version and reflects cultural shifts in US society: for example, homosexuality was included as a disorder until 1973. It was then removed to represent the more current view that it is a normal preferential variation of sexuality (a view that is still disputed by some, usually religious, professionals in the USA). The current version is number IV, but you can find interesting discussions on the web about the production of number V.

What we think of as normal or as abnormal behaviour is dependent on the cultural context of the behaviour. Children in different cultures may share common developmental stages but how we describe these and how parents respond to and care for their children varies significantly. If children in different cultures, such as middle-class white America and impoverished rural India, have very different experiences of life, this raises a question about whether a construct like ADHD, described and defined in the former country, will still apply in the latter. What we regard as 'normal' behaviour in children is very varied. (What teachers regard as acceptable behaviour certainly varies within and between classrooms and schools.) Perhaps it is unreasonable to expect young children to sit silently and passively in class for long periods: in many European countries, indeed, children remain at nursery school until the age of 7. We should also recognise that there will be a wide range of characteristics and developmental stages in any class, and some children will be more likely to sit still and focus on literacy and numeracy than others.

So ADHD is a 'disorder', originally just in children but now also in adults, that is identified through a behaviour checklist from the DSM IV (for full checklist see http://www.adhdfamilyonline.com/public/239.cfm). Although there is a large research body of evidence of neurological difference, ADHD can still not be identified by medical tests but is diagnosed on the basis of behaviour alone. The neurological research identifying brain differences has been criticised since much of it involves children who are already on medication (Leo and Cohen, 2003). ADHD is a highly contested idea; there is disagreement about its existence as a discrete measurable disorder and a single entity. Despite this, it is diagnosed at increasing rates worldwide and the medication associated with the diagnosis is a multi-billion-dollar industry (Lloyd and Norris, 1999; Cohen, 2006).

ADHD: a subjective diagnosis
ADHD has no clear physical signs that can be seen in an x-ray or laboratory test. It can only be diagnosed by looking for certain characteristics of behaviour. These include levels of inattention (difficulty in

concentrating), hyperactivity (disorganised, excessive levels of activity) and impulsive behaviour which are considered 'developmentally inappropriate'.

Inattention

- have a hard time keeping their mind on one thing/get easily bored
- may give effortless attention to things they like
- but focusing deliberate conscious attention on organising or completing a task is difficult

Hyperactivity

- always in motion, can't sit still
- dash around or talk incessantly
- squirm, wriggle, roam, touch everything, tap

Impulsivity

- unable to curb reactions
- don't think before action
- may blurt out comments

To meet the criteria, symptoms must:

- have started before age 7
- have persisted for at least six months
- be pervasive (more than one of home, school, socially)
- have caused significant functional impairment
- not constitute other 'mental disorders'.

There must be clear evidence that symptoms interfere with, or reduce the quality of, social or academic functioning.

It should be apparent that these are behaviours which typify large numbers of children, young people and adults, even perhaps ourselves. They may be inconvenient but are not particularly abnormal. Even with the final set of requirements, they may not necessarily be symptoms of an underlying medical or psychological disorder.

We do not know how many children in the UK are diagnosed with ADHD as the numbers are not recorded, but we can see how rapidly prescriptions for ADHD medication have increased. This information is collected by the National Health Service as much of the medication used is methylphenidate, a form of amphetamine (a class B drug if used illegally) which must therefore be recorded.

Between 1997 and 2009 there was a more than sixfold increase in the number of prescriptions for methylphenidate in England, to the point where, in 2009, 610,000 prescriptions were issued (Hansard, October 2011). The Guidelines produced by National Institute for Health and Clinical Excellence (NICE), (SIGN in Scotland) estimate that up to about 9 per cent of children have 'mild to moderate' ADHD whilst 1 per cent are listed as 'severe' (NICE, 2008). As there is no objective measure however, and since prevalence varies hugely between health boards, this is really an estimate based on the US figures. The number of families receiving Disability Living Allowance for children with severe behaviour problems has also increased rapidly over recent years (Stead and Lloyd, 2008).

ADHD in the early twenty-first century: why now?

There are a number of features of current life that might be associated with the very rapid spread of ADHD. The first is the increased exposure in other countries to US information about the DSM and ADHD through the internet. Parents and professionals can access this information directly and easily. There are now an enormous number of websites that describe and discuss ADHD; some of these sites are those of parent support groups which are financed by pharmaceutical companies.

In the early 1990s pharmaceutical companies in the USA anticipated that their US market for methylphenidate was becoming saturated so new markets needed to be found. They began to market intensively in the UK and Europe. In the USA drugs like methylphenidate can be directly advertised in magazines with adverts aimed at parents. The drug companies compete with each other to persuade parents to buy their particular drug. These adverts often come with pictures of smiling successful children with a sales pitch that suggests that their particular drugs could improve academic performance or 'deliver results that matter'. In the UK such advertisements were aimed at the medical profession (Lloyd and Norris, 1999) and led to an immediate increase in diagnosis and medication.

ADHD: what causes it?

There are real concerns on the part of some parents and professionals about the behaviour of children and young people. While every generation believes their children are more badly behaved and lacking in respect than their elders (Munn *et al*, 2011), current concerns are worth considering. Why might some of the present generation of young people show the kind of behaviour associated with the ADHD label? The medical answer lies in biological inheritance; other explanations draw on a varying mix of biological, environmental, psychological and/or social factors.

Biological explanations suggest that ADHD involves a problem in response inhibition due to abnormalities in brain function which have a genetic element (Kewley, 1999). Other brain-based explanations focus on the idea of faulty 'executive functions' (Barkley, 2005). However, a range of psychosocial and social factors might also make sense of the ADHD phenomenon, including changing family patterns; the influence of diet, drugs and alcohol; educational factors and information, marketing, funding and financial support. It may be particularly important to consider the fast society we now live in, and the exposure of children and young people to *fast media* including some television programmes and computer games.

There have been major changes in social and community structures in Western societies, with the decline of manufacturing industries and changing employment patterns for men and women. Safety concerns have reduced many children's participation in free, unstructured and energetic play in the open air (Armstrong, 2006). New mass media involve 24-hour TV, electronic games, and visual exposure to real and virtual violence. Armstrong argues that we should see ADHD as a symptom of contemporary cultural issues: 'the so-called ADHD child's behaviours reveal much more about the culture that we live in than about the specific mechanisms that reside within an individual brain' (Armstrong, 2006:34). Television from earlier times seems much slower. Programme makers and advertisers now assume that viewers have a very short attention span and need fast frequent changes. This is particularly noticeable in some US-based children's cartoon channels as well as computer games targeted at adolescent boys.

Children's behaviour may also be related to their experience of family life. There are families who find it difficult to care for their children, families where there is abuse, violence or neglect, and families where there has been a difficult separation from a parent – though it is difficult to say whether this is more prevalent now than it was in previous times. Children and young people who are in care, particularly those who have experienced multiple failures of the care system, often show this kind of behaviour. Children whose mothers have used alcohol or illegal drugs while pregnant often have difficulties, as might children who live in polluted environments, whose diet is inadequate or who have food intolerances. The widespread use of some food additives may also be relevant.

ADHD also came to prominence at a time of educational change in many countries. In the USA and UK there were changes in classroom practice associated with the pressure for early achievement, a concern for standards and national testing. Formal teaching began earlier and there was a reduction in the informal and creative aspects of the curriculum such as drama. Some children find it more difficult than others to settle down to this passive mode of learning for large parts of the school day. Even those who do not react in a 'hyperactive' manner may still not be comfortable with long periods of inactivity. It is an easy step to interpret their restlessness as bad behaviour and then transform it into a medical disorder: labelling 'unwanted conduct as disease' (Whitt and Danforth, 2010).

ADHD is a complex individual and social phenomenon

It is clear from the above that there is a wide and complex range of reasons why any individual child might show this kind of behaviour. It seems too simple just to say, 'They behave like this because they have a disorder'. We need a sophisticated understanding that begins with the realities of individual children's lives and not with a psychiatric label.

Labels like ADHD can detract from the individuality and complex humanity of children and limit our expectations of their abilities to manage their lives. The diagnosis can make parents feel supported; it can be a 'label of forgiveness' for those who had felt blamed by schools for their children's difficulties. It can lead to educational and possibly psychological support. It might make people pay attention to the child's needs. It can lead to medication that may benefit some children. It might also lead to better learning support for schools and additional income for families.

However, such labels can also make the behaviour seem inevitable, a syndrome or disease more difficult to change. A diagnosis often means that other reasons for the child's behaviour are left unexplored. It can mean teachers think they need special knowledge in order to support the child. On their part, the children can feel they are unable to change their behaviour – 'it's because I've got ADHD.'

Focusing on the behaviours of the individual 'problem child' or adolescent can also deflect teachers from thinking more creatively about how they might introduce more active forms of learning into their classrooms. Many pupils might benefit from forms of learning which depend less on the transmission and absorption of knowledge and more on active engagement in problem-solving and design.

Is medication the answer?

There are three types of medication prescribed in the UK. Methylphenidate is the most frequently prescribed medication (commercial names include Ritalin, Concerta and Equasym) but there is also dextroamphetamine (Dexedrine) and atomoxetine (Strattera). Many children also receive further medication for sleep problems or depression. There are a number of serious concerns about the use of medication for behaviour considered to be ADHD.

That some children feel helped by medication is not altogether surprising; methylphenidate was given to World War II fighter pilots to improve their concentration (British Psychological Society, 1996), while many US college students believe legally, or more often illegally, sourced methylphenidate helps them study.

However a number of concerns surround the use of medication for behaviour considered to be ADHD: there are concerns about the scale and rapidity of increase in prescriptions worldwide, concerns that such prescriptions may be given without sufficient consultation and/or monitoring (Stead and Lloyd, 2008), and concerns that the dose which effectively manages behaviour in school means children are understimulated. Side effects of methylphenidate can include sleep and eating problems, stomach pains, growth defects, dizziness, headaches, tics, suicidal thoughts and 'behavioural rebound' (where the withdrawal from medication leads to the behaviour getting worse).

Although a large number of studies have investigated the use of methylphenidate in relation to ADHD, very few long-term studies have been conducted in this area. There are major concerns about the impact such powerful brain-altering medication has on the child's developing brain. Brains continue to develop throughout childhood and into adulthood. If early life experiences shape their neuronal and organisational connections, this raises questions about whether the use of psychoactive medication on children negatively affects critical learning phases and what some psychologists have called windows of opportunity for particular cognitive development (Derrington *et al*, 2003).

Nerve connections are also promoted when glucose is stimulated by physical activity. The increasingly widespread prescription of methylphenidate to reduce activity may, paradoxically, reduce the development of the cognitive processes needed to promote a child's attention and help them manage their behaviour. There are also concerns about the prescription of medication to children who are younger than the recommended age. Furthermore, a connection with the later use of other psychotropic (mind-altering) substances has now been firmly established.

Graham cites recent longitudinal research from Australia which indicates that *ever* receiving stimulant medication increases the odds of a child 'being identified as performing below their age-level by a classroom teacher by a factor of 10.5 times' (Smith *et al*, 2010, cited in Graham, 2010).

Did this girl have ADHD?

She couldn't concentrate on one thing at a time, didn't listen, was very easily distracted. She didn't finish her sentences and interrupted others. She frequently forgot her homework and school equipment, lost her schoolbooks and was very often late for school. She was disorganised and impulsive.

This was me. I was always in trouble for forgetting things, was often bored in class and used to read novels under the desk.

Did I have a disorder? No, it was just the way I was. Did it interfere with my learning? In some ways, yes. Did I need help? Yes, I needed help and advice as to how to manage myself and my learning better, but did not get any. Schools, including mine, often failed to recognise the range of individual differences in their students. But at least I wasn't subjected to an ADHD diagnosis and medication.

I am now a successful academic. I have written many articles and books and was head of a large university department. I travel widely. I am a parent and grandparent. I still talk too fast, interrupt people and am impulsive, but I have had a good life. This is just the kind of person I am. I learned to manage my life. I could have learned this a lot faster if schools had been aware that many children need help to work out how they learn best and how to organise their learning and their lives. Now I keep a notebook, I make lists, I use notes and sticky labels as reminders. I learned to listen to people. I recognised that my inability to do one thing at a time means that I can multi-task! While writing this chapter I stopped occasionally to search for flights and look up suitable climbing plants for my garden. That is how I often work – I have learned to work to my strengths so now when I need to concentrate I can. Children with the behaviour associated with an ADHD diagnosis can learn too.

Children with ADHD type difficulties can be helped to learn

Perhaps the most important place to start is with the realisation that children labelled ADHD are not all the same! They are individual human beings with very different experiences of life. They will have different family and parenting experiences. They will have had different educational experiences and different learning support. They will be in different class groups and different peer groups. They may be living in poverty – statistics presented to the Scottish Parliament on patients seeing doctors about ADHD indicate that the highest numbers came from the most deprived areas (Stead and Lloyd, 2008).

They may be lively, open and overactive. They may be quiet and withdrawn. They may or may not be on medication. They will usually be boys but also sometimes girls, of different ages and with different interests. They may have very different preferences for how to learn; some may prefer to work in quiet places while others may prefer white background noise. They may work best alone or in groups or informal settings. They may be motivated by quite different things. They will represent a wide range of human diversity and should not be seen only through a label that refers to some difficulties they may show. They need an individual educational plan that builds on their strengths and interests. Reid argues that it is helpful to begin with an observation and analysis of how the student acts and learns in the classroom and offers an Interactive Observational Style Inventory that helps the teacher think about different aspects of the student's learning and behaviour (Reid, 2006).

There is a multiplicity of books for teachers that offer the so-called answer to teaching pupils with ADHD. Many of these offer simplistic definitions of ADHD as a disorder and give lists of advice. It is interesting to realise, once you have read a number of these books, how similar the advice is to the generality of advice given to teachers about classroom and behaviour management. The advice below, for example, comes from an ADHD support website:

> Classroom rules should be clear and concise and reviewed regularly with the student. It is helpful to have the child repeat back rules, expectations or other instructions to make sure they are understood. These rules should be posted prominently in the classroom. (Low, 2011)

Advice about classroom management tends to reflect the general advice that is offered to young teachers about clarity of expectations, simple clear rules negotiated with the class and a range of strategies which promote and encourage positive behaviour (Munn *et al,* 2011). Reward is more effective than punishment in changing behaviour in school; it is helpful to focus on positive behaviour, recognise strengths and achievements, promote social skills, empathy and peer group relationships and encourage the possibility of self-change.

Approaches like restorative practice encourage empathy and an understanding of the consequences of actions, and can resolve classroom difficulties without psycho-pathologising pupils (McCluskey *et al,* 2011). They allow teachers to reframe their view of what they regard as problem behaviour. Teachers can step back and consider the frame or lens through which this reality is created and try to understand the unspoken ideas or framework through which they make sense of it – they can try, in other words, to think of alternate ways of making sense of the child's behaviour.

There are many possible ways to organise classroom learning that will lead to thoughtful engagement and active response. Students can be engaged in activities where they identify their own solutions and help construct their own programmes. Metacognitive skills of problem-solving, visualisation and organisation could also be taught more explicitly in classrooms and would be of help to many students. If some have difficulty following instructions, keep the instructions simple, remind the students and preview (eg. 'in five minutes I will ask you to finish your work and put it away'). Make sure they have heard the request – get them to repeat it. If it's complicated get them to write it down. Helpful reminders to avoid organisational problems and forgetfulness can be given through the use of home school diaries or notes, personal notebooks, lists, sticky labels and reminders about equipment.

Physical activity produces the glucose necessary for brain development. Research in the USA found that physical exercise programmes reduced ADHD-type behaviour (Wendt, 2000). Building short spells of physical activity into lessons could benefit many children. Nor should we simply assume that all children must do the same things at the same time.

Parents often feel unfairly blamed for their children's actions and a label like ADHD can make them feel absolved of this. However, it can also make them pessimistic about change and more likely to reach for medication. School can support parents and understand their difficulties, even when they may feel that parents sometimes contribute to them. Parents, carers and teachers can work effectively together to develop common strategies to support children and respond to challenging behaviour. They can form and share an understanding of the complex, individual humanity of the student.

Summary
A diagnosis of ADHD can lead to a diminished view of the child's possibilities. There are many concerns about the risks of medication. Some

children have real difficulties for a complex range of individual, family, social and educational reasons. But not all of them have a neurological disorder. In my view we should pursue as far as we can all possible means of supporting children and young people with challenging behaviour without recourse to a medicalising of childhood. But with or without a diagnosis and label, teachers can make a difference to their lives by a thoughtful and creative use of educational strategies that value them as learners.

Suggested watching

Ken Robinson, 'ADHD: The tonsillectomy of the 21st Century?' http://www.youtube.com/watch?v=HlnN7t4Zl04

Further reading:

Graham, Linda J (2010) *(De)Constructing ADHD: Critical Guidance for Teachers and Teacher Educators.* New York: Peter Lang

Lloyd G, Stead, J and Cohen, D eds (2006) *Critical New Perspectives on ADHD.* Abingdon: Routledge

---

References

American Psychiatric Association (2000) *Diagnostic and Statistical Manual of Mental Disorders, Fourth Edition, Text Revision.* Washington, DC: American Psychiatric Association

Armstrong, T (2006) Canaries in the coal mine. In Lloyd, G, Stead, J and Cohen, D (eds) *Critical New Perspectives on ADHD.* Abingdon: Routledge

Bailey, S (2009) Producing ADHD: an ethnographic study of behavioural discourses of early childhood. PhD thesis, University of Nottingham

Barkley, RA (2005) *Attention-Deficit Hyperactivity Disorder: a handbook for diagnosis and treatment* (3rd edn). New York: Guilford Press

British Psychological Society (1996) *A Psychological Response to an Evolving Concept.* Leicester: British Psychological Society

Cohen, D (2006) Critiques of the 'ADHD' enterprise. In Lloyd, G, Stead, J and Cohen, D (eds) *Critical New Perspectives on ADHD.* London: Routledge

Derrington, T, Shapiro, B and Smith, B (2003) *Brain Development: the connection between neurobiology and experience.* Hawaii: University of Hawaii Center on Disability Studies

Graham, L J (ed) (2010) *(De)Constructing ADHD.* New York: Peter Lang

Kewley, G (1999) *Attention Deficit Hyperactivity Disorder.* London: David Fulton

Leo, J and Cohen, D (2003) Broken brains or flawed studies. *The Journal of Mind and Behaviour* 24(1) p29-56

Lloyd, G and Norris, C (1999) Including ADHD. *Disability and Society* 14(4) p505-517

Lloyd, G, Stead, J and Cohen, D (eds) (2006) *Critical New Perspectives on ADHD.* Abingdon: Routledge

Low, K (2011) *School tips for ADHD,* http://add.about.com/od/childrenandteens/a/adhd-classroom.htm (accessed 2 Nov 2011)

McCluskey, G, Lloyd, G, Kane, J, Riddell, S, Stead, J and Weedon, E (2011) Teachers are afraid we are stealing their strength. *British Journal of Educational Studies* 59(2) p105-119

Munn, P, Sharp, S, Lloyd, G, Macleod, G, McCluskey, G, Brown, J and Hamilton, L (2011) A comparison of staff perceptions of behaviour in Scottish schools in 2009 and 2006. *Research Papers in Education*

NICE (2008) *Attention Deficit Hyperactivity Disorder (ADHD)* (CG72). London: National Institute for Clinical Excellence

Reid, G (2006) Managing attention deficit difficulties in the classroom: a learning styles perspective. in Lloyd, G, Stead, J and Cohen, D (eds) *Critical New Perspectives on ADHD.* London: Routledge

Smith, G, Jongeling, B, Hartmann, P, Russell, C, and Landau, L (2010) *Raine ADHD Study: long term outcomes associated with stimulant medication in the treatment of ADHD in children.* Government of Western Australia Department of Health.

Stead, J and Lloyd, G (2008) ADHD: creating continuing dilemmas for education in Scotand. *Scottish Educational Review* 40(1) p42-54

Vallee, M (2011) Resisting American psychiatry: French opposition to DSM-III, biological reductionism, and the pharmaceutical ethos. In McGann, P J and Hutson, D J (ed) *Sociology of Diagnosis (Advances in Medical Sociology, Volume 12).* Emerald Group Publishing Limited

Wendt, M (2000) *The effect of an activity program designed with intense and frequent physical exercise on the behaviour of ADHD children.* Buffalo: State University of New York

Whitt, P B and Danforth, S (2010) Reclaiming the power of address: new metaphors and narratives for challenging behaviour. In Graham, LJ (ed) *(De)Constructing ADHD.* New York: Peter Lang

12

Gypsies, Roma, Travellers: teachers making a difference

Gillean McCluskey and Tess Watson

Introduction

This chapter sets out to help teachers working with pupils from Gypsy, Roma and Traveller (GRT) communities, perhaps for the first time. Teachers want to do their best for all children in their care but sometimes it can be difficult to know what to do, what to say, and how to understand the needs of new children when faced with the unexpected. The aim of this chapter, therefore, is to help you think about what it would be helpful to know so that, whether the arrival of a new pupil is planned or unexpected, you can help them to make the most of the teaching and learning in your school.

The chapter begins by offering some background information on GRT communities in the UK today. It then explores some of the language and vocabulary used in talking about children from GRT communities and the ways in which this is changing. From there it moves on to explore their experiences in education and the outcomes they currently achieve. Next the chapter outlines two case studies to help you reflect on practice. These case studies are based on the views of teachers who used their reflections on recent research together with their professional experience to make a difference for pupils from GRT communities. Finally we offer a summary of the main points for reflection and action for you in your school.

As a teacher it is likely that at some point you will have one or more pupils from the GRT communities in your class. It may not happen often, depending on the location of the school, and you may not necessarily be aware of it when it does. So you may wonder why a whole chapter is devoted to examining how teachers can best support pupils who may only be seen occasionally. By way of response, the experiences of pupils from GRT communities have much to teach us about social justice and can help us reflect not just on their particular experiences but on broader lessons about the ways in which many minority groups experience education in the UK.

What do we mean when we talk about 'Gypsy', 'Roma' and 'Traveller'?

Recent thinking in the field of race relations makes it clear that 'race' is a political rather than biological term and indeed that it is racist to suggest that there are typical personal qualities which have an assumed biological basis. You will see discussion of this thoughout this book. Although the terms GRT and Traveller are used for convenience in this chapter, this does not imply that everyone is predictably the same or that all members of GRT communities have the same views and practices. As in all groups, there are different views and approaches to key issues within GRT communities, which depend on factors such as age, gender and so on.

Several different communities of Gypsies, Roma and Travellers currently live in the UK. In England and Wales Gypsy Travellers are sometimes called Romanies or 'Romany chals'. In Scotland they might be called Gypsy Travellers, Tinkers or 'Nawkens' or 'Nachins'. Irish Gypsy Travellers are also sometimes called Tinkers. Some of these words like Gypsy or Tinker may be used with pride by Travellers but can also be used as terms of abuse by settled people.

These communities have often been in this country for many generations. They are partly descended from groups of people who most likely left India hundreds of years ago and travelled through Asia and Europe. In Europe these people are now often referred to as Roma; in France they are known as Tsiganes and in Germany, Sinti. The Roma communities in Europe have often been persecuted over the centuries, which led to their near destruction during the Holocaust where probably around half a million or more were subjected to medical research and killed in the concentration camps (United States Holocaust Memorial Museum).

In the UK, groups of Romanies arrived over several centuries, meeting and mixing with groups of other Travellers on the roads. Although it is difficult to get accurate figures, some estimates suggest that there are around 25,000 to 30,000 Gypsies, Roma and Travellers in Britain today, including several thousand in Scotland. This figure includes groups of Show and Fairground Travellers, also known as occupational Travellers. Occupational Travellers largely see themselves as a business community and do not claim ethnic minority status.

The language of GRT in different parts of the UK includes Romani words as well as those that reflect the cultures of the part of the country they have travelled in. For example Scottish 'cant' includes Gaelic words. Other groups in Britain include European Roma, many of whom are from Eastern Europe where since World War II they have often been subject to forced settlement and children have been disproportionately educated in special schools. In recent years some European countries have seen a notable increase in prejudice and violence towards Roma.

The term Gypsy, Roma, Traveller is now used more widely in the UK than, say, Gypsy or Traveller and aims to convey this complex situation with greater accuracy. In mainland Europe the term Roma is increasingly prevalent and often refers to all these communities. It is worth noting that debates are ongoing within and outside the GRT communities which concern these matters. GRT communities often have rich and diverse oral traditions but have rarely written about their own histories, culture or lifestyles. It is important to acknowledge that accounts of their lifestyles and linguistic and cultural heritage, such as the one in this chapter, tend to be written *about* them, rather than *by* them.

Where are the GRT pupils?

It has always been difficult to get accurate information about the numbers of GRT pupils in schools. Fear of being stereotyped and bullied has often led pupils from these communities to choose to 'pass' as settled ('gadgie' or 'gorgo') children, so official figures are likely to be an underestimate (Lloyd and McCluskey, 2008). Making themselves invisible has perhaps been a protection but it has also allowed the prejudice against them to continue and, some would argue, to intensify (Themelis, 2009). This can be seen, for example, in some of the inflammatory media coverage of the evictions of families at Dale Farm in 2011.

It has always been the case in the past that some children enrolled in primary schools attended school for part of the year and travelled with their families for work the rest of the time. Fewer enrolled in secondary schools and often did not stay on until the age of 16. Sometimes they lived in houses, or in trailers on sites and sometimes on unofficial encampments, on the roadside for example. This seems to be changing now as many more families stay in houses or semi-permanently in trailers and travel less. A common confusion for non-Travellers is to think that because a family lives in a house or does not travel, they are not real Travellers or have stopped being Travellers. This is not the case. Many continue to have great pride in their identity as members of GRT communities, and value their family and community histories of travelling life, family-based learning, story telling, economic independence, self-employment and traditional practical crafts and skills that have been handed down through generations. They very much see themselves as Travellers.

Anecdotal evidence suggests that increasing numbers of parents are keen to enrol their children in school, especially at primary stages. The technological advances of recent years may be partly responsible for this, as parents see the link between new work and business opportunities and school-based achievements and attainment. There is also evidence that many young GRT pupils have very positive attitudes to school and increasingly high expectations, despite the fact that many teachers continue to have low expectations of them (Wilkin *et al,* 2009).

Official statistics show an increase in the numbers of GRT pupils who continue into secondary education (though again these are likely to be inaccurate) but figures are still lower than in primary. Reasons that account for this are often complex but they may relate in part to worries about a child's personal safety and the likelihood that they will experience verbal or physical abuse. Explanations may also relate to differing cultural values; for example, GRT parents may see the teaching about sexual health and relationships as the responsibility of the family rather than school. Other aspects of the curriculum may be seen as irrelevant, especially as it is common for boys to take on adult roles earlier in GRT communities and to become involved in work and business from the age of 12 or 13. There is also sometimes a fear that important family and cultural values will be diluted or lost by attending secondary school.

So you are more likely to meet children from GRT communities if you work in primary school and the children are more likely to be in your school throughout their schooling than in the past. If you work in secondary schools, you are more likely to meet girls and young women than boys.

What are the key issues for GRT pupils in schools?

It is useful to understand the larger context for Gypsy, Roma and Traveller pupils in education. Key concerns relate to two discrete but related aspects of experience:

- the continuing underachievement of GRT children in UK education systems, and the longitudinal data from national statistics which indicate that they comprise the lowest-achieving minority group in education overall in the UK (Wilkin *et al*, 2009)

- the identification of Roma as the most vulnerable and deprived minority ethnic group within Europe (Halász, 2007).

This context is important. It can act as a reminder of the link between the child you may have in class and the larger patterns of disadvantage encountered by children from a particular group or community.

Underachievement remains a major issue. While primary school attendance has increased, rates of achievement are still very low when compared with those other groups and communities. Literacy rates are particularly low. While it may be argued that success and achievement are culturally determined concepts in education, and that practical skills and financial independence have traditionally been more important to GRT families, there is no doubt that raising literacy levels opens the doors to a wider range of educational and employment opportunities, especially in the current economic climate. National statistical data points to serious concerns about attainment levels (DCSF, 2008).

As a teacher you may have heard about inappropriate behaviour among Traveller pupils and their high rate of exclusion from school.

However research into exclusion from school among GRT pupils found that such exclusions often resulted from fighting or violence which arose out of harassment and bullying in school (Lloyd and Stead, 2001). More recent research mirrored this finding and highlighted the continuing problem of racist abuse for GRT pupils (Archer and Francis, 2007).

There is no evidence that GRT pupils are any more or less troublesome in school than other pupils. Behaviour is generally good, especially among younger pupils. There is evidence that they may experience more difficulties in their relationships with both staff and pupils. Sometimes the open and direct style of GRT pupils has been misinterpreted as rudeness. Outside school the same style may reflect the well-developed skills of negotiation and self-efficacy which are needed to build up business and work opportunities. Teachers know the importance of building on pupils' own interests and starting points and knowing how to interpret such assertiveness may provide a good basis for more positive interaction overall.

The context of larger patterns of disadvantage may be particularly relevant for teachers working to support new arrivals from Roma communities in Eastern Europe. Although these children may have some aspects in common with previous asylum seekers, refugees and other pupils who have English as an Additional Language (EAL) needs, there may be new and significantly different challenges facing many of the families. These concerns centre on the following: poor and erratic attendance, poor and erratic attainment, low overall levels of pupil engagement with school and low parental engagement with school, eg. at school meetings, parents' nights and school-arranged social events. Issues of poor and overcrowded housing often compound these issues.

Families have often come from countries where Roma have been persecuted, discriminated against or forced to assimilate for generations. Living conditions for the majority of Roma in Europe are mostly very poor compared to other groups; they have higher unemployment rates and lower life expectancy. This forms a backdrop to the experiences of many children arriving in UK schools. One of the case studies below looks at how teachers in one school have worked to help Roma children settle and build strong relationships with home, sometimes in quite challenging circumstances.

In summary, the key issues for children across different kinds of GRT communities are:

- low rates of attendance
- high rates of disciplinary exclusion
- racism
- low teacher expectations
- underachievement
- reluctance to self-identify for fear of discrimination.

Schools and teachers have become increasingly effective at tackling these issues and overcoming barriers to learning. The case studies outlined below are based on real accounts of experience. They come from teachers who have developed practical ways to ensure that issues of social justice are at the forefront of their practice. All the teachers who kindly passed on their ideas advise against trying to implement them wholesale. It is always important to think about your own teaching context: the school catchment and community, the overall characteristics of pupils, advice from any recent inspections or reviews and so on. It is also helpful to remember how long it can take to embed change in a school.

The following case studies are the result of thinking carefully about context; about the micro-climate of the classroom and the macro-climate of society and the patterns of disadvantage discussed earlier. As you read through the stories, we invite to think about how you would adapt the ideas for your own situation. Both schools used in the case studies are located in Scotland.

Case study 1

The school studied is a mainstream primary school of average size in a large urban area in Scotland. It has a very high percentage of pupils who are bilingual and multilingual. It has a high number of pupils who are recent arrivals from Eastern Europe. In 2004/05, 17 per cent of pupils were Roma but by 2009/10, 51 per cent of pupils were from Roma families. The challenges for the school in this situation were many: building trust with the new community was clearly important but so too was recognising that there were tensions with the local community. Teachers rapidly became aware that attendance and education were not seen as priorities by most of the new arrivals. They also saw a number of pupils with health issues. This put strain on teachers and their morale declined in the face of financial cutbacks and the impact this had on support and resourcing. The attention needed to support high numbers of children in every class who spoke no English also gave rise to concerns about the need to maintain and raise attainment levels for more established pupils. There were also behavioural issues.

The school team, led by its headteacher, began to devise ways of meeting the children's needs. To address the challenges, they:

- found out more about the background of the Roma community
- developed a major arts project to encourage parents to mix
- supplied school uniforms
- arranged for an interpreter to attend the school breakfast club once a fortnight – where parents could drop in
- arranged more formal parents' meetings with the local council diversity officer and health worker (with interpreter)
- had the school senior leadership team make home visits to address attendance issues
- developed a close working relationship with the police diversity officer and community health worker
- encouraged parent involvement in events such as a 'school values' week, International Week, the school launch of the Children's Charter and community clean-ups
- used an online tool http://newarrivals.segfl.org.uk/, with translation capability, to help with enrolment
- ensured that the school handbook refers specifically to its anti-racist commitment within the curriculum and within its discipline policy.

In daily practice around the school, there has also been a focus on building a positive shared ethos. The senior leadership team in the school are involved in playground monitoring to encourage integration but, just as importantly, older pupils who have been in school for longer, but who also arrived in school from new European Union countries, have been trained as playground buddies to help children mix. An emphasis on playground games and lunchtime football have also made a difference. A new behaviour policy, with a focus on an explicit set of values, has been developed in consultation with pupils and a strong focus on celebrating achievements has been maintained and further developed.

Within the classroom, challenges have been addressed in various ways. A tiered system of support for learning has been introduced. Older pupils from new EU countries spend time with the youngest pupils in what is called the 'learning room'. A system of learning partners in class has worked very well for pupils. Support from the local council has enabled the school to find new resources which match the interests of new arrivals but which are suited in language and vocabulary to the level of their developing literacy skills in English.

Many strategies which are effective for all learners also work well for new arrivals, and include active learning, formative assessment and a home reading club run by the EAL teacher. Sometimes it has been difficult for teachers to assess whether a child needs support from the EAL service or has more complex barriers to learning which may include developmental delay. A language base was set up to assist pupils but had to close because of funding problems.

Despite the hard work of the school and its team of teachers and support staff, challenges remain: new, less experienced staff have come into post; a new school leadership team has taken over; questions about setting by ability for maths and language are being debated; and awareness has re-emerged of the need for a continuous evaluation of the needs of pupils and staff. Griffiths (2003) asks us to think about social justice as a verb not a noun; as a process rather than a simple target to be met and overtaken. The work of the school team here exemplifies just that understanding. They recognise that the challenges will continue and this is part of what it is to be a strong school community.

Case Study 2

There are many different ways that pupils from GRT communities engage with schooling and outside urban areas, arrangements may need to be very different from those described in Case Study 1. In another part of the local council area, schools have been working with GRT families who have a long history of association with the area. This area has a large number of commuter towns and some scenic rural areas but some parts still have significant multiple deprivation. While some GRT families live on a local council site, others live in houses. Teachers knew that families had concerns about bullying and discrimination and suspected that the children, especially as they grew older, were self-excluding from school as a result. They also had concerns about pupils not being able to access an appropriate curriculum during times away travelling.

To meet the challenges here has also required a very flexible approach. Two designated teachers for GRT families support the children with interrupted learning. One has a background in primary teaching, the other in secondary teaching. Both recognised that young people, including GRT children and young people, have developed very good IT and virtual networking skills and realised the importance of utilising these skills. The teachers aim to help pupils:

- learn about GRT cultures, values and priorities
- provide netbooks for families when on the move
- provide direct teaching for 4-6 hours a week in a portacabin on site
- provide PCs in the portacabin for pupils' use
- commit to blended learning
- use personal virtual folders made accessible through the national online learning community website
- build up individual support plans with pupils
- take a mobile community education bus to visit the site weekly to assist with special needs and additional support
- welcome GRT pupils who live in houses and on the site on the bus
- make contact through mobile phone and via post when pupils are away travelling
- provide a base in local libraries where secondary-aged young people can work towards national qualifications.

There are still barriers to making this work well and one particular concern has been the use of netbooks. As part of local council policy on child protection, the netbooks have been modified with a firewall to ensure there is no access to sites such as You Tube or social networks. While this may be understandable, it may also limit pupils' ability to develop and extend understandings of the wider world and mean they continue to see school work as separate from their own interests and priorities. This is part of an ongoing debate within the context of interrupted learning but it also takes place more generally in schools as well as among many teachers. The low overall level of academic attainment is also a continuing concern though there are some indications that improvement is slowly being made.

Other local councils have provided portacabins on GRT sites for pupils in an acknowledgment of the fact that the expectation to attend school can in itself be a deterrent to engagement with learning and achievement. The portacabin has proved to be a neutral and safe place for teaching and has allowed stronger communication between education services and families to be built over time. The provision of an identified teacher who links home and the formal education system has often been seen as valuable by GRT families. However there is clearly some way to go in thinking about social justice for all when some pupils feel so unsafe in school that this is seen as the best way to provide education.

Summary

This chapter has outlined some of the context for Gypsy, Roma and Traveller pupils in education. The two case studies describe some effective approaches to thinking about social justice in schools for children and reflect on some of the key lessons learned by teachers. Cultural dissonance describes the 'sense of discomfort, discord or disharmony arising from cultural differences or inconsistencies which are unexpected or unexplained and therefore difficult for individuals to negotiate' (Derrington and Kendall, 2004). Learning about GRT culture and priorities has clearly helped overcome this cultural dissonance for teachers in these settings to some extent.

An emphasis on shared understanding, respect and high expectations has also been essential. It is worth remembering that research repeatedly indicates that teacher expectations and attitudes are a very important determinant of what happens for pupils in a class. Positive attitudes by teachers are known to be hugely significant to achievement in its broadest sense.

Research also suggests that strong peer relationships between GRT and other pupils helps reduce the numbers of GRT pupils leaving school earlier than they normally would (Derrington and Kendall, 2004). This reminds us of the ways in which social and academic learning are often intertwined. The role of partnership working is also evident in these case studies, despite their very different approaches. Again, research suggests that inter-agency collaboration is a necessary key strategy to achieve equality of access, opportunity and outcomes. Eliciting change for the better takes time. Thinking about social justice is an important part of making positive change happen. The experience of the teachers described here shows that this process is rarely straightforward and often complex, but by combining findings from research with professional experience, teachers can be ready to meet these challenges and ensure their classrooms are welcoming to all.

Further reading

Attewell J, Savill-Smith C, Douch R (2009) *The Impact of Mobile Learning: Examining what it means for teaching and learning* (LSN Learning, Making Learning Work)

Wilkin, A, Derrington, C and Foster B, (2009) *Improving the Outcomes for Gypsy, Roma and Traveller Pupils: Literature Review* (DCSF Research Report 077). London: DCSF

References

Archer, L and Francis, B (2007) *Understanding Minority Ethnic Achievement in Schools*. Abingdon: Routledge

Department for Children, School and Families (2008) *The Inclusion of Gypsy, Roma and Traveller Children and Young People*. London: DCSF

Derrington, C and Kendall, S (2004) *Gypsy Traveller Students in Secondary Schools: culture, identity and achievement*. Stoke on Trent: Trentham Books

Griffiths, M (2003) *Action for Social Justice in Education: fairly different*. Buckingham: Open University Press

Halász, K (2007) *The Situation of Roma in Europe*. Brussels: Directorate General for Employment and Social Affairs of the European Commission, European Union

Lloyd, G and McCluskey, G (2008) Education and Gypsies/Travellers: 'contradictions and significant silences'. *International Journal of Inclusive Education* 12(4) p331-345

Lloyd, G and Stead, J (2001) 'The boys and girls not calling me names and the teachers to believe me', *Children and Society* 15(5) p361-374

Themelis, S (2009) Questioning inclusion: the education of Roma/Traveller students and young people in Europe and England – a critical examination. *Research in Comparative and International Education* 4(3) p262-275

United States Holocaust Memorial Museum website accessed 3.5.12 http://www.ushmm.org/wlc/en/article.php?ModuleId=10005219

Wilkin, A, Derrington, C and Foster, B (2009) *Outcomes for Gypsy, Roma and Traveller pupils: literature review*, DCSF-RB077. London: DCSF

For more information about Gypsy, Roma and Traveller communities go to the STEP website at http://www.scottishtravellered.net/

13

The twenty-first century teacher needs to engage with race and racism

Rowena Arshad

Despite the many publications about race equality in school education over several decades, student teachers, qualified teachers and senior managers continue to say that they find this a difficult area to address and feel ill-prepared (Lander, 2011; Arshad *et al*, 2005). This is partly due to the minimalist way in which race equality has been addressed in teacher education (Wilkins and Lall, 2010; Bhopal *et al*, 2009; Hick *et al*, 2011), with the consequence that white teachers in particular are 'conditioned not to think about race' (Marx, 2006:21). With increasing diversity in society and the classroom, it is important for teachers to get over any hesitation about race and racism so that they develop the confidence and capacity to engage in discussion with young people. Unless they do so, phrases like 'getting it right for every child' will be empty slogans, particularly for the pupils who encounter racism or racial discrimination as part of their lives.

This chapter aims to clarify concepts related to race equality work, debunk some incorrect assumptions and provide ideas for practice.

Clarifying concepts

Robin Richardson, an experienced adviser in equalities work, suggests (Richardson, 2003) that the phrase 'race equality' is generally used in two ways. The first is as a moral value or principle. Therefore we seek to

193

educate for race equality because we believe that all human beings are of equal value and that it would be wrong to discriminate because of an aspect of someone's race. Under the Equality Act 2010, the definition of race includes colour, nationality, ethnic origins and national origins.

The second way the phrase is used is where race equality is viewed as a measurable outcome. Achieving race equality would mean reducing any gaps between people of different racial groups in employment, educational achievement and so on.

It could be argued that both uses of the phrase are necessary if we are to be effective. There is a need to educate all pupils to see beyond labels and stereotypes, to explore what people have in common and where they differ, to have opportunities to engage in learning activities that help them think about racism, inequality, prejudice, discrimination and human rights and so on. Equally, to evaluate for equality of opportunity, we need to monitor how the education system is meeting the needs of pupils from different backgrounds. However, while monitoring attainment, school attendance and exclusions can provide us with statistics, it is questionable whether we can actually measure *race equality*.

It might be useful here to pause and consider this term race. This is a term which comes from historical attempts to categorise people according to their skin colour and physical characteristics. It is therefore a socially constructed term, without scientific basis and in itself somewhat meaningless. Individuals, not races, are the main sources of human variation. The word race is used with quotation marks by some academics and practitioners as an acknowledgement that it is a contested term. It is now more common to see the term *ethnicity* being used when discussing people of different 'racial' backgrounds. While ethnicity is also a socially constructed concept, it takes the discussion wider than race, which has tended to be based on aspects of physical appearance, such as colour, or on supposed genetic ancestry. The House of Lords, in passing judgement in Mandla v Dowell Lee on 24 March 1983, stated that some of the key criteria for defining an ethnic group would include a long shared history and a common cultural tradition. In addition, there may also be a common geographical origin, language, literature or religion.

However, rather than getting caught up in which is the correct term to use, since terminology is always changing, it is important that teachers concentrate on developing critical lenses through which to discuss issues of racism and power. This means developing a questioning voice when considering matters related to race/ethnicity: for example, to ask whose voices are heard and whose are not, whose viewpoints are presented as common sense or correct and whose are not. Let us consider some issues in the curriculum. In literature or music, the classics are largely portrayed as coming from Europe. Did the other big civilisations of Asia, the Middle East and Africa not produce great literature and music too? When teaching about Christopher Columbus's voyages to America, are discussions also developed about the indigenous peoples' perspectives and how they had their rights eroded through European colonisation? Even the notion that Columbus 'discovered America' suggests that nobody was there before him, or perhaps that they did not matter. What sources are provided that tell the story from the viewpoint of indigenous peoples, and not as discovery but as conquest?

When engaging with race equality, we need to focus on how to provide pupils at each age and stage and within different subject areas with a more complete and accurate understanding of the world in order to help young people to become critical and reflective learners.

From assimilation to multicultural education to antiracist education
Others have written in greater detail about the different approaches to race in education over the decades (Troyna, 1993; Gillborn, 2008). I briefly describe some of these approaches to stimulate debate and discussion.

The dominant approach from the 1950s to the late 1970s was an *assimilationist* model. According to this philosophy, ethnic minorities were expected to leave behind their distinctive identity in order to fit in with the values, attitudes and behaviours of the dominant group or culture. The term was often used to describe the process of immigrants fitting into their new country by adopting its customs and habits – 'when in Rome do as the Romans do'. In schools, this involved discouraging pupils from speaking any language other than English and parents were even advised to discourage their children from speaking other languages than English at home. The rationale behind this was that these pupils would learn English faster and assimilate into their new culture but this proved not to be the case.

It was eventually recognised that the assimilationist approach tended to imply a negative attitude to the minority – a deficit perspective – and policy-makers and teachers began to adopt the *multicultural* model. It was hoped that this might foster greater interaction, integration and harmony by enabling people to learn about different cultures, faiths, languages and ethnicity. Teachers were largely comfortable with adopting a multicultural approach, for example by celebrating different festivals such as Chinese New Year, Eid, Divali or Hanukkah, wearing different clothes, learning a different cuisine, and trying out the dance, music and lifestyles of those the majority group considered to be 'other'.

However, multicultural education also had its critics. Barry Troyna famously called it the 3 Ss – saris, steelbands and samosas. For Troyna, the multicultural approach, though well-intentioned, tokenistically sprinkled ethnic diversity onto an otherwise unchanged curriculum. Such an approach also avoided discussions of racism or racial discrimination (Troyna and Williams, 1986). Troyna complained that multicultural education was more about lifestyles than life chances. He did not believe the lives of minority ethnic pupils would improve much as a result of multicultural education.

Another weakness was that multicultural education tended to essentialise and reify cultures, presuming each culture to be static, a fixed thing you can teach about. It was often quite superficial, focusing for example on religious ritual and sacred objects rather than understanding the complexity of ways of life and social beliefs as they moved from one part of the world to another. Multiculturalism assumes that individuals have to choose which particular culture to adopt. In reality, cultures evolve and change all the time, and many people have a mix of cultures and identities.

Those who saw the limitations of multicultural education argued for *antiracist* education, which would challenge racism more directly. Such an approach would help pupils understand and deal with racism, prejudice and stereotyping. Unlike *multicultural* education it would deal with issues of power, justice and inequality and address issues of racism within the formal and hidden curricula. The focus was not on becoming more sensitive towards minority cultures but on the processes and effects of racism, including how it manifested within school-level education.

Antiracist education was never taken up with the same fervour as multicultural education, and many teachers actively resisted this approach. There may be several explanations for this. Firstly, the approach is more political, shifting the gaze away from the way of life of minorities to the attitudes and actions of the majority, and highlighting differences of social power between majority and minorities. It directly questioned whether the mainstream curriculum could adequately meet the needs of a diverse pupil population. So many teachers found it easier and safer to stick to celebrating cultures at a fairly superficial level, as unusual or exotic.

Secondly, there has never been clear policy guidance for teachers, at least in Scotland, on how to take antiracist education forward. Teachers have few opportunities to effectively engage with this approach or consider workable strategies and ideas for implementation and so the uptake of the antiracist approach has been ad hoc and minimal.

Others have claimed that the divide between multicultural and antiracist education is unhelpful and that both approaches are needed. For example, a multicultural approach might be appropriate with younger children, so that they accept diversity as normal. As they grow older, they can be introduced to antiracist education and learn to recognise racism and be confident at challenging it. Those who advocate this mixed approach remind us that multiculturalism is important but insufficient, and that too often those who begin with multicultural education fail to progress their thinking or develop antiracist activities in the curriculum.

Others believe that neither the multicultural nor the antiracist approach is sufficient, and advocate another approach which they call 'critical multiculturalism' (May, 1999; May and Sleeter, 2010). Critical multiculturalism 'gives priority to structural analysis of unequal power relationships, analysing the role of institutionalised inequities, including but not necessarily limited to racism' (May and Sleeter, 2010:17). In other words, it highlights and challenges various kinds of prejudice and power, and relates the experience of race to issues of gender and class.

This approach is not as well known in Britain as in the United States, and until recently there have been few practical ideas offered on how it can be implemented. May and Sleeter 2010 suggest a range of methods for raising teachers' awareness of discrimination and structural inequalities, for example organising for student teachers to work with families from marginalised communities so that they can develop greater understanding of issues which these families face. It suggests critically examining what the dominant ideologies are in the education system. For example, a physical education teacher might discuss the 'racialised constructions of thin, white bodies', or a music specialist critique 'Eurocentric structures and assumptions that are embodied in school music programs' (May and Sleeter, 2010:20). In science the teacher could apply a post-colonial lens to critically examine how indigenous knowledge from different parts of the world has been interpreted or silenced. May and Sleeter are not confident that this approach will become popular in the UK or the US as, just like antiracist education, this approach is likely to disrupt and destabilise the status quo.

It is important to appreciate the differences between these approaches in order to reflect on everyday practice in schools and classrooms and to bring about worthwhile change. The next section aims to strengthen this reflection and development by looking at some incorrect assumptions that can stand in the way of teachers engaging with race equality.

Debunking some incorrect assumptions

Race equality only matters in schools with minority ethnic pupils

This view is not uncommon, and assumes that race equality is only relevant for minority ethnic pupils. A study of minority ethnic pupils' experiences of going to school in Scotland, involving interviews with 82 teachers, found that few teachers saw the benefits for majority ethnic pupils or for themselves as teachers. The teachers viewed education for race equality as something that one did to benefit minority ethnic pupils.

In less diverse schools the issue of race can be seen as less relevant or important, but it might actually be more important. Schools which do not have ethnic, linguistic, religious or cultural diversities among their pupils have few resources with which to counteract stereotyping or incorrect assumptions about other groups. Research repeatedly provides evidence that mainly white schools do not adequately prepare their pupils for adult life in a society that is culturally and ethnically diverse (Donald *et al*, 1995; Cline *et al*, 2002; Arshad *et al*, 2005).

It is discriminatory to see difference

Some teachers adopt a 'colour-blind' approach where they pretend not to notice or care about issues of colour or ethnicity. The assumption here is that 'we treat everyone the same' and that to notice colour or ethnicity is to hold some kind of prejudicial attitude or engage in a pre-judicial act. Colour and ethnicity have historically been used as divisive categories and, in the eyes of some teachers, it is better not to mention them but to look instead for the individual qualities and traits of each child, paying little attention to their cultural background. These quotations illustrate this attitude:

> We don't see the colour of the child, we see the child. (Deputy Headteacher, Primary, quoted in Arshad *et al*, 2005: 67)

> I mean to be honest, I don't classify children by language or race or religion. I just accept the children as they are and we don't enquire closely into what nationality, what religion and so on and that's true of the white population as well ... I think our strength is that we treat them the same ... (Teacher, Secondary, quoted in *ibid*)

This interpretation of being fair extends to other aspects of school life:

> I don't think we make any special effort to encourage minority ethnic parents onto the school board because we treat everybody the same. (Deputy Headteacher, Primary, quoted in *ibid*)

Yet teachers do need to develop an analytic understanding of the impact of difference and how difference is perceived, especially when some sections of the population have more power and influence or higher status than others. How else might the needs of every child be met in a practical way? Moreover, if difference is not seen or valued, how can the rich mix of backgrounds of pupils, parents and communities be drawn upon as a resource for educating young people and developing them as citizens?

The confusion for white people about whether it is better to speak about race or stay silent has been the subject of some interesting research. Bridget Byrne (2000), interviewing white mothers in London about child-rearing, found that they were generally anxious not to be seen to be racist and believed that the simplest way not to appear racist was to avoid talking about race. Byrne described how difficult it was for her interviewees to sustain a discussion about issues of race. She also commented on the irrelevance of race issues to white lives. In contrast, these interviewees had no problems discussing gender. She concluded that seeing racial differences appeared to be much more contentious and complicated than seeing gender differences. She also suggested that it is easy for white people to avoid acknowledging visual racial markers but that black people cannot. In addition, the white mothers of mixed-race children informed her that their children had relatively complex responses to colour differences.

But we have done race ... that is no longer the real issue

Others do not talk about race as they feel it is both overemphasised and not the most significant marker of difference. Yet there is research to show that teachers, largely white and middle-class, tend to under-appreciate the impact of everyday racism that minority pupils and their families may be experiencing (Equality Commission for Northern Ireland, 2003; Caulfield *et al*, 2005; Arshad *et al*, 2005).

Such a response illustrates a simplistic view of what race equality means. The absence of racist incidents or bullying does not prove the absence of racism or the presence of race equality it simply means that no incidents have been reported or recorded.

It is helpful to return to Richardson's suggestion that race equality is a moral value or principle. If we as teachers wish to educate the citizens of tomorrow not to judge people because of the colour of their skin, their ethnicity, faith, language or culture, then we need to establish opportunities within the curriculum and within the whole school that help young people to acquire the necessary knowledge. The report from the Stephen Lawrence Inquiry explicitly calls on the education system from pre-school upwards to have specific and coordinated action to raise awareness about racism and to promote a greater valuing of cultural diversity (Macpherson, 1999: Chapter 6, paras 6.54-6.56).

Different forms of racism

Teachers who want to 'get it right for every child' need to understand what racism means and how it can manifest itself on a daily basis within school. Racism is the ideology that one race is superior to another. This notion of superiority is then applied to and embedded in the structures, practices, attitudes and beliefs that we operate within. In the past, racism has generally been viewed as a black/white issue based on skin colour. While a lot of historical racism was related to colour (eg. slavery), there were other forms of racism which were based on ethnicity, nationality and culture, often interwoven with religion. Jewish people, Gypsies/Travellers, and the Irish who came to settle in mainland Britain encountered this form of racism. As we move into an age of super-diversity, we need a broader sense of racism which, while still acknowledging colour racism, extends to culture, ethnicity and religion (Mac an Ghaill, 1999).

We also need to consider how racism plays out on a day-to-day basis. Racism can appear in several, often interrelated, forms. Thompson (2011) suggests that we can consider this at three levels – personal, cultural and institutional.

Personal racism comes from 'our thoughts, feelings and actions at an individual level' (Thompson, 2011:25). It can have a significant effect in reproducing inequalities, particularly if the individual holding such views is in a position of power. Examples of personal racism include:

- being racially abusive/harassing
- engaging in physical attacks
- allowing personal assumptions, prejudices or stereotypes on racial issues to influence decisions regarding recruitment and selection of staff or students
- condoning a culture which tolerates racist language and jokes in the workplace.

One example of open and explicit personal racism would be if a teacher blatantly disliked Gypsy, Roma, Travellers, and viewed them as scroungers and treated GRT pupils as unworthy of respect. Most people who engage in personal racism do so without realising it. For example, if you are surprised that some Asian families can speak 'good

English', this suggests a degree of unacknowledged ignorance and possibly racial prejudice, which might affect how you relate to Asian pupils or parents.

Cultural racism arises when a particular culture perceives itself as superior to others. It is often when one culture is dominant that cultural racism can become systematic. The dominant culture then imposes its patterns, assumptions and values on others, often in a manner that many do not even notice. This becomes the common-sense culture, taken for granted as part of everyday life. The use of derogatory language is one way in which one cultural group asserts its power over another, with discriminatory outcomes. In some parts of the UK you will hear it argued that using words like 'Paki' or 'Chinky' is not discriminatory since this is part of the local vernacular, yet these are words which many minority ethnic groups regard as offensive. Challenging these terms can be met with resistance but this does not mean they are acceptable. Multicultural education and cultural diversity programmes open the way for strategies for challenging cultural racism.

The common definition for *institutional racism* in the UK is derived from the Stephen Lawrence Inquiry Report:

> The collective failure of an organisation to provide an appropriate and professional service to people because of their colour, culture, or ethnic origin. It can be seen or detected in processes, attitudes and behaviour which amount to discrimination through unwitting prejudice, ignorance, thoughtlessness and racist stereotyping which disadvantage minority ethnic peope. It persists because of the failure of the organisation openly and adequately to recognise and address its existence and causes by policy, example and leadership. (Macpherson, 1999: Chapter 6, para 6.34)

An example of institutional racism would be a school that refuses to acknowledge that racism can occur there and takes no action to address it. Antiracist education/training is a preferred strategy for addressing institutional racism.

Transforming practice

Teachers who are serious about being inclusive and transformative educators need to engage in what Howard calls the 'three sides of the Achievement Triangle' (Howard, 2006:128). The three sides are (i) to know yourself; (ii) to know your pupils and (iii) to know your practice. These should be familiar areas to many teachers who aspire to be reflective and reflexive practitioners.

In terms of race equality, this would involve a critical examination of your own values and thinking related to matters of racial difference: how much do you know about the issues, what are your gaps in knowledge and whose voices influence your thinking? There is research to show that white teachers in particular are anxious about placing race on the learning and teaching agenda because many of the issues are not part of their experience (Gaine, 1995; Cline *et al*, 2002).

> I think there is a problem in society as a whole, but it doesn't touch my life personally. I would welcome staff development or some form of training because I feel a bit at sea ... because it's not something I've really thought much about before. (Headteacher, Primary, quoted in Arshad *et al*, 2005:168)

How well do you know your pupils and their views on issues of difference and diversity? It is known that minority ethnic pupils often comment on their teachers' ignorance of cultural and religious backgrounds (Cline *et al*, 2002; Caulfield *et al*, 2005; Arshad *et al*, 2005). Teachers themselves are well aware of this gap in their knowledge. It is difficult to provide a single route map of how this knowledge gap might be reduced but acknowledging that gaps might exist is a good start.

It would be dishonest for a teacher to dismiss any review of their practice by arguing that they already treat people fairly and are committed to equality of opportunity. There is always room for improvement.

There has been a lot written over the decades to provide teachers with practical ways of promoting race equality. It can be considered as part of subject areas or as an explicit topic, and both approaches are needed. A quick internet search would provide ideas for every age and stage and subject area. I end this chapter with some ideas, which will hopefully stimulate you to search for others.

- The ability to speak more than one language should be valued and encouraged. Read Learning in 2+ Languages (http://www. ltscotland.org.uk/resources/l/genericresource_tcm4530612.as p?strReferringChannel=search&strReferringPageID=tcm:4-615801-64).

■ Curricular inputs relating to race equality should be contemporary as well as historical. Pupils can learn, for example, about the efforts of Martin Luther King but also about those of the parents of Stephen Lawrence in the UK. Studies on the Civil Rights movement should link to explorations of forms of racism in the UK.

■ Citizenship programmes on race equality can be developed progressively through each group: for example, exploring issues of belonging will ensure that issues of faith, ethnicity, colour and national origin are explicitly discussed. Resources suitable for age and stage are used, eg. Persona Dolls (http://www.persona-doll-training.org/ukhome.html) in the early years; *Throwing Stones* DVD (http://www.throwingstones.org.uk/) for upper primary and lower secondary.

■ Religious events should be taken into account when planning school trips, lessons and activities; pay attention to both recognising and celebrating as well as making necessary adjustments and provision. (See the SHAP Calendar of Festivals at http://www.shapworkingparty.org.uk/calendar.html.)

■ Badger Books (www.badger-publishing.co.uk) are a resource for the early years. You can request their books under themes like celebrating difference, positive images, faiths and festivals collection, and challenging racism through literature.

■ Drama can be used to raise issues of racism, Islamophobia and sectarianism. Go to www.ltscotland.org.uk and search for 'race equality'.

■ In Physical Education, you can provide opportunities to discuss how issues of racism prevent participation and fairness.

■ In Art, a range of cultural perspectives can be taught.

■ In Maths lessons, statistics can be used that alert pupils to race-related issues: examples could be racial harassment statistics, diversity in population demographics, and the most recent Census data.

■ Science lessons can actively debunk myths about the hierarchy of 'races' and explore scientific reasons behind different types of skin colour.

- A resource for curricular inputs on human rights/children's rights is *Children's Rights: a teacher's guide* by Save the Children (http://www.savethechildren.org.uk/resources/online-library/childrens-rights-a-teachers-guide); a resource for education for co-operation and conflict resolution is *We Work Together: can you?* available from the Citizenship Foundation (http://www.citizenshipfoundation.org.uk/main/resource.php?s170).

- The physical environment of your classroom can give out a clear message of promoting diversity and stamping out prejudice, ignorance, discrimination and bigotry. These messages ideally should be developed through posters and pupils' work, and these displays could be in different languages to demonstrate the diversity of languages spoken in the school.

- A range of learning and teaching methods can be used to involve pupils in consideration of and discussion about diversity e.g. role play, drama, blogs, investigations, research projects, discussions, interviews, speakers, poster making, Circle Time activities, story books, novels, songs and poetry.

- Literature (eg. Malorie Blackman's book *Noughts and Crosses*) can be used to open up discussions on race equality and challenge stereotypes.

- The achievement of black and minority ethnic individuals, both contemporary and historical and across the professions, should be given due credit in subject lessons.

- Using development/global education materials, pupils can explore race equality within the UK as part of studying and discussing issues in the wider world.

- Some useful international sites for teachers include Racism no-way – an Australian site with teaching resources and discussion (http://www.racismnoway.com.au/); Multicultural pavilion – a US site full of ideas and strategies (http://www.edchange.org/multicultural/); Rethinking Schools – another US site (http://www.rethinkingschools.org/index.shtml – type in race equality or racism) and Teachers College Record (http://www.tcrecord.org/) – a further US site with scholarly articles about a range of social justice issues including race.

■ Useful websites for secondary-age young people on race, racism and growing up in Britain are Britkid (www.britkid.org) and Coastkids (www.coastkid.org). For global information on human rights, poverty and refugees, visit Cyberschoolbus (http://cyberschoolbus.un.org/).

Further Reading

Journal of Race Equality Teaching – this is a practitioner's journal issued three times a year for teachers interested in embedding race equality into their work. It is published by Trentham Books.

Gaine, C (2005) *We're All White Thanks: The Persisting Myth About 'White' Schools*, Stoke on Trent: Trentham Books

---

References

Arshad, R, Almeida Diniz, F, Kelly, E, O'Hara, P, Sharp, S and Syed, R (2005) *Minority Ethnic Pupils' Experiences of School in Scotland (MEPESS).* Edinburgh: Scottish Government, http://www.scotland.gov.uk/Resource/Doc/920/0033758.pdf

Bhopal, K, Harris, R, and Rhamie, J (2009) *The teaching of race, diversity and inclusion on PGCE courses: a case study analysis of University of Southampton.* Multiverse, TDA

Byrne, B (2000) Troubling Race: using Judith Butler's work to think about racialised bodies and selves. In *Queering Development*, IDS Seminar series, http://www.ids.ac.uk/files/dmfile/byrne.pdf

Caulfield, C, Hill, M and Shelton, A (2005) *The Experiences of Black and Minority Ethnic Young People following the Transition to Secondary School.* Glasgow: Scottish Council for Research in Education

Cline, T, Abreu, G de, Fihosy, C, Gray, H, Lambert, H and Neale, J (2002) *Minority Ethnic Pupils in Mainly White Schools. Research Report RR365.* London: Department for Education and Skills

Donald, P, Gosling, S, Hamilton, J, Hawkes, N, McKenzie, D and Stronach, I (1995) 'No problem here': action research against racism in a mainly white area. *British Educational Research Journal* 21(3)

Equality Commission for Northern Ireland (2003) *Equality Awareness in Teacher Education and Training in Northern Ireland.* Belfast: Equality Commission for Northern Ireland, http://arrts.gtcni.org.uk/gtcni/bitstream/2428/6344/1/Equality%20awareness%20in%20teacher%20education %20and%20training%20in%20NI.pdf

Gaine, C (1995) *Still No Problem Here.* Stoke on Trent: Trentham Books

Gillborn, D (2008) *Racism and Education: coincidence or conspiracy?* London: Routledge

Hick, P, Arshad, R, Mitchell, L, Watts, D and Roberts, L (2011) *Promoting Cohesion, Challenging Expectations: educating the teachers of tomorrow for race equality and diversity in 21st century schools*, http://www.ceres.education.ed.ac.uk/wpcontent/uploads/Race equalityandteachereducation24.pdf

Howard, G R (2006) *We Can't Teach What We Don't Know: white teachers, multiracial schools.* New York: Teachers College Press

Lander, V (2011) Race, culture and all that: an exploration of the perspectives of White secondary student teachers about race equality issues in their initial teacher education. *Race, Ethnicity and Education* 14(3) p351-364

Mac an Ghaill, M (1999) *Contemporary Racisms and Ethnicities: social and cultural transformations.* Buckingham: Open University Press

Macpherson of Cluny, Sir William (1999) *The Stephen Lawrence Inquiry* (Macpherson Report). London: TSO

Marx, S (2006) *Revealing the Invisible: confronting passive racism in teacher education.* Oxford: Routledge

May, S (1999) *Critical Multiculturalism: rethinking multicultural and antiracist education. London: Routledge*

May, S and Sleeter, C (2010) *Critical Multiculturalism: theory and praxis.* London: Routledge

Richardson, R (2003) Removing the barriers to race equality in education: ten points to think and talk about. Paper presented at conference 'Steps for Promoting Race Equality in Education', Brunei Gallery, London, 10 June, http://www.teacherworld.org.uk/Articles/Robin-1.htm

Thompson, N (2011) *Promoting Equality: working with difference and diversity.* Basingstoke: Palgrave Macmillan

Troyna, B (1993) *Racism and Education.* Buckingham: Open University Press

Troyna, B and Williams, J (1986) *Racism, Education and the State: the racialisation of educational policy.* London: Croom Helm

Wilkins, C and Lall, R (2010) Getting by or getting on? Black student teachers' experiences of teacher education. *Race Equality Teaching* 28(2)(Spring) p19-26

Some final thoughts

Terry Wrigley, Rowena Arshad, Lynne Pratt

Teaching is a profession of hope. It involves the formation of each new generation into the citizens of tomorrow, for a world that is not yet known. We do not know what the future will look like, but we do know that what happens in classrooms today will help to shape it. We hope this book has demonstrated how important teachers are in helping to achieve greater inclusion and justice in the world.

We hope that the chapters have connected with the everyday realities of classrooms and relate to the dilemmas you face. Not all of them will have been easy to read, because of the complex issues they deal with. We believe that reading and re-reading them will help you develop a clear understanding to interpret and navigate the diverse situations of real schools and classrooms. In this age of 'super-diversity', it is difficult to categorise or place people into neat boxes. It is therefore all the more important for us to sharpen up our thinking and practice by developing a critical understanding of issues of difference.

There are some key messages that emerge from this book which we hope readers will reflect upon.

The first is that education is not a neutral exercise. The fact that something is normal, standard practice and officially sanctioned does not make it right. The policy makers who speak in terms of 'delivering' a ready-made package of knowledge distort the reality of teaching and learning, and undermine the ethics of the teaching profession. The role of the teacher involves ethical engagement and never simply a search for more effective transmission.

Decisions are made by governments, education policy makers and those in positions of power about the types of knowledge to impart and what is considered useful knowledge. Therefore, as teachers concerned about social justice, we need to develop forensic skills which allow us to question whose knowledge is being taught or not taught, whose perspectives are dominant and whose are being silenced, and what our role as teachers is in helping learners, whatever their age and stage, to become the critical thinkers of tomorrow.

Some education systems have a rigid view of the curriculum while others are more open. In every context, however, teachers have decisions to make on what to emphasise, which perspectives to highlight, how to interpret the official curriculum and how to develop a critical understanding of the world.

All these decisions are taken with an eye on the realities of our students' lives and their present understandings. This goes beyond a sense of making learning *relevant*, in the simple sense of young people's current experience and interests, and involves engaging with their *concerns* about their own lives and those of others. We always need to ask how the curriculum as it is actually taught provides the great diversity of pupils with the knowledge and tools to develop a sense of their own worth in society, an understanding of how injustice occurs, and a capacity to challenge discrimination against themselves and others.

The second is the importance of seeing the bigger picture. In the everyday reality of schools and classrooms, there is understandably a strong focus on helping the individual child towards inclusion and achievement. However the focus on what can be done for the individual pupil runs the danger of inadvertently buying into a deficit model. This model locates the problem within the individual pupil rather than seeing that the barriers a person might face could lie in the way educational institutions and social structures are organised. Such a deficit model risks stigmatising individual pupils rather than focusing on the institutional or cultural barriers to participation and recognition. It seeks answers through assimilating individuals into an existing environment, rather than questioning whether the environment is socially just.

The third key message is that to be a teacher for social justice you do not have to be a superhero. Many teachers who have a commitment to social justice start with small practical steps in their classroom. This might involve working with a pupil who is underachieving or who is perceived as 'other'. The response might entail small changes in practice, but to ensure that we do not fall into the trap of an individualised or deficit view, we need to move on to more thoughtful reflection about values, language and power. These small steps serve as powerful reminders that all teachers can make a difference and contribute to the transformation of their immediate learning environment.

Some teachers may go on to influence changes at school level or in wider society but the important point is that they acted and were not simply compliant. It is a mistake to make too strong a distinction between the little changes which an individual teacher can bring about and those which require high-level managerial decisions. A small group of concerned teachers can have a major impact on a whole school; good practice in a school can gain recognition; and teachers can build networks on a wider scale with others who share particular concerns.

The title of this book is *Social Justice Re-examined*, which implies that something has already changed. In the 21st century, crude forms of discrimination are largely recognised and understood by teachers. It is our belief that no teacher would tolerate overt forms of discrimination, injustice and bullying and most would find a way to address such incidents.

However, the everyday forms of discrimination – the subtle forms that often go unrecognised by those not on the receiving end – still exist and when these are pointed out, there are various possible responses. One not uncommon reaction by teachers is disbelief that such things could still happen in this enlightened and inclusive age. Another is to feel daunted by the complexity of it all, or to avoid raising difficult issues out of embarrassment or politeness. Around issues where discrimination is condemned by law, some teachers might ensure that their practice complies with the letter of the law but neglect to reflect more deeply on what is happening below the surface. We hope this book will help its readers think more deeply and that you will return to some chapters again and again.

It is difficult to explain subtle forms of exclusion, marginalisation or discrimination as these will play out in different forms depending on the combination of characteristics. For example, if lessons about women's achievements highlight able-bodied and prosperous white women, then girls who are disabled or from an ethnic minority or working class background will not be receiving strong cues about their identity and worth. This is an example of bias by omission. If allowed to continue over time, the cumulative impact can be to make many pupils invisible in the school and curriculum. No malice is involved in such omission but there will be a serious impact.

Schools have many functions. They are places where young people develop skills which will help them earn a living. They provide an initiation into leisure interests and diverse forms of cultural activity. They are an educational space which provides time and resources and guidance for reflecting on the norms and values of the wider society, as well as enabling young people to speak up for justice.

While we have been concentrating on the pupils, it is important to be mindful that you cannot have an inclusive school where the teachers themselves do not feel valued and heard. An inclusive school is a place where all (pupils, teachers, parents, community, visitors) are accepted in their individuality and difference and a place where there is a duty of care for each other within an ethos of respect. Social justice is about all of these dimensions and purposes.

We hope that teachers and student teachers who read the book will become empowered or re-energised to help create a different and more just future and continue to find reward and joy in teaching.

Notes on Contributors

Rowena Arshad is the Head of the Institute for Education, Community and Society, School of Education, University of Edinburgh. She has over 30 years working with educators on social justice issues, particularly on 'race' equality. Her current research focus is on issues and areas connected to theme of meeting the challenges of super-diversity in the classroom and society.

Shereen Benjamin taught in primary, secondary and special schools in London for 12 years. She is now a senior lecturer in primary education at the University of Edinburgh, where she teaches student teachers and examines the effects of intersecting inequalities on educational experiences and attainment.

Akwugo Emejulu is lecturer in Community Education at the University of Edinburgh. She has research interests in two areas: investigating ethnic and gender inequalities in a comparative perspective and exploring expressions of political identity and agency within the micro-politics of community development and community organising. Her work has appeared in *Politics and Gender, the Community Development Journal* and *Interface*. She is currently working on a cross-national research project exploring how the economic crisis is impacting on minority women's grassroots-based activism in France and the UK.

Yvonne Foley is a Lecturer in Language Teaching at the University of Edinburgh. She has been an EAL/ESL teacher and teacher educator in Taiwan and the UK. Yvonne's research interests focus on exploring teachers' beliefs about the reading needs of EAL pupils; language teacher education, teacher identity; and critical literacies.

Andy Hancock is a lecturer in Primary Education at the University of Edinburgh. He has many years experience working as a teacher in multilingual classrooms in England, Scotland and Zimbabwe and as a manager of a local authority Bilingual Support Service.

Helen Knowles is a Primary School Teacher and has been teaching for five years. She has worked in three primary schools in Scotland and has taught a spread of different classes throughout the schools, including some Support for Learning work. She is particularly interested in gender.

Gwynedd Lloyd is an Honorary Fellow at the University of Edinburgh and an independent researcher/consultant. She has researched and written widely about troubled and troublesome young people, behaviour at school, and ADHD. She is often quoted about ADHD in the media and has spoken about it in different countries.

Ann MacDonald taught in the primary sector in Scotland for 16 years, predominantly in early years settings. She is currently a lecturer in Primary Education at the University of Edinburgh, where she is Programme Director for BEd Primary (Hons). Her research interests include gender, religion and the lives of women teachers.

Gillean McCluskey is a lecturer and Associate Director of the Scottish Traveller Education Programme, based in University of Edinburgh's School of Education. Her main research is in school discipline, exclusion, disaffection, restorative practices and the issues for those on the margins in education. She has worked as a teacher in mainstream schools and alternative settings with young people in trouble and at risk.

Ian Menter (AcSS) is Professor of Teacher Education and Director of Professional Programmes in the Department of Education at the University of Oxford. He previously worked at the Universities of Glasgow, the West of Scotland, London Metropolitan, the West of England and Gloucestershire. Before that he was a primary school teacher in Bristol, England.

Laura Mitchell works at the University of Edinburgh with undergraduates and post-graduates, focusing primarily on how to embed social justice within teaching practice. Prior to this post Laura worked in the City of Edinburgh Council, where she was mainly responsible for implementing policy and practice to address discrimination in schools.

Lynne Pratt is the Programme Director for the PGDE Secondary in the School of Education, University of Edinburgh. Her principal interest is in primary children's creative writing and meta cognition. Lynne has a particular interest in using children and young adult literature to assist student teachers engage with social justice. Lynne was a secondary school teacher of English.

Paul Vernell is Head of English at Abbeywood Community School in South Gloucestershire where he has taught for over 23 years. Paul has written several articles on education including *Is another school possible?* with Chris Carter in *Socialist Review* Sept 2008. Paul is also Joint Secretary of the South Gloucestershire Division of the National Union of Teachers.

Tess Watson is teacher of Science. She has taught for twelve years and her experience includes both Primary and Secondary sectors and Additional Support Needs (ASN). Tess has a special interest in how new and emerging technologies can enhance teaching and learning and support mobile learning. During her teaching career she has also been seconded as a Mobile eLearning Pilot Project Manager and an Education Support Officer.

Terry Wrigley is Visiting Professor at Leeds Metropolitan University and Honorary Senior Research Fellow at the University of Ballarat. He was previously Senior Lecturer at the University of Edinburgh, working in teacher education and on issues of social justice. He edits the international journal *Improving Schools.* His books are: *The Power to Learn* (2000), *Schools of Hope* (2003), *Another School is Possible* (2006) and *Changing Schools: Alternative Ways to Make a World of Difference* (eds, 2012). He is currently working with John Smyth on a new book about the impact of poverty and social class on education.

Subject Index

Name Index